Phyllis Korkki

WITHDRAWN

T H I N G

How to

Complete Your

Creative Project Even

If You're a Lazy, Self-Doubting

Procrastinator Like Me

HARPER

An Imprint of HarperCollins*Publishers*

HarperCollins books may be purchased for educational, business, or sales promotional use. For information, please e-mail the Special Markets Department at SP sales@harpercollins.com.

FIRST EDITION

Designed by Fritz Metsch

Library of Congress Cataloging-in-Publication Data
Names: Korkki, Phyllis, author.
Title: The big thing : how to complete your creative project even if you're a
    lazy, self-doubting procrastinator like me / Phyllis Korkki.
Description: First edition. | New York, NY : Harper, [2016]
Identifiers: LCCN 2015050620 (print) | LCCN 2016006277 (ebook) | ISBN
    9780062384300 (hardback) | ISBN 9780062472588 (audio) | ISBN 9780062384324
    (ebook)
Subjects: LCSH: Creative ability. | Success. | Motivation (Psychology) |
    Procrastination. | BISAC: BUSINESS & ECONOMICS / Motivational.
Classification: LCC BF408 .K6595 2016 (print) | LCC BF408 (ebook) | DDC
    153.3/5--dc23
LC record available at http://lccn.loc.gov/2015050620

---

16 17 18 19 20   OV/RRD   10 9 8 7 6 5 4 3 2 1

To my parents

Contents

Introduction

I've wanted to write a book since I was eleven. I wasn't quite sure what it would be about, but it churned vaguely in my mind for about four decades, causing a long-running psychic discontent.

Then a few years ago I wrote a column about deadlines for the *New York Times*, where I work. Using the column itself as an example of the power of deadlines, I noted that I didn't really get started on it until I announced to my coworkers that I planned to write it and told them exactly when I planned to hand it in.

Unwilling as I was to write the column—how could I possibly do the topic justice?—I completed it on time because I had a deadline. I met the deadline because I would have let my coworkers down and endangered my reputation if I hadn't.

That column got me wondering: How could more people, including me, approach long-term personal projects with that same sense of urgency? That's when, after a little over forty years of gestation, the topic of my book became clear. The Big Thing of the title refers to a major project that is personally meaningful and requires sustained effort to complete. It requires us to create a unique structure that comes into view slowly as we focus on the individual pieces of it, time after incremental time.

With a Big Thing, we don't normally face the same stakes that we do on the job. We may be too shy to tell other people about our creative goal, so no one even knows to expect something. If we do tell others, they may show polite or even genuine interest. But these people are not going to demand that we hand in our project at a certain time. That's what makes it so hard.

But that's also what makes it so important. Big Things aren't decided by employers or clients. They come from deep inside us, and reflect our personal talents, values, and points of view. They are a way for us to order our experience, and to connect and amplify the moments of our lives. But too often they remain obscured by the demands and distractions of everyday life, and by fears of failure.

How, I wondered, can people raise the importance of their Big Things in their own minds to the point that they actually pursue and complete them? Maybe, I thought, I could find the answer by writing this book.

Like that column on deadlines, this book is a "meta" book. It is a big creative project about the desire and struggle to complete big creative projects. This conceit—both in the sense of "ingeniously contrived" and "having or showing an excessively high opinion of oneself"—makes me a little uncomfortable. But I decided that the best way to approach this topic would be to live it myself, and to analyze not only my own experience but that of many others who have pursued Big Things. On the way, I'll debunk some myths about creativity, go down some quirky and unexpected paths as I tie creativity to the human condition, and provide insights from myself and others.

Some people insist that you should only create if you can't *not* do it—that the creative fire must burn so intensely that you feel driven to work on your project at all costs. Others say you must have an iron will and work on your project each and every day at a set time, whether you feel inspired or not. I'm here to say that this is simply not true. Only a small percentage of the population possesses that kind of inner fire and discipline.

The rest of us with big creative dreams may be intermittent and unsure in our attempts. We may procrastinate and make excuses and allow ourselves to be distracted by more fleeting concerns. But the goal in our minds still has value, and in our own way we are committed to it. So how can we remove the obstacles that prevent us from achieving it?

In the course of my research, I met and learned about creative people who did have that unrelenting fire. Many others did not, and yet they still managed to persist with their projects. I talked to people who endured major obstacles—things like mental and physical illness, severe sleep disorders, and addiction. I also met people who faced the common challenges of self-doubt, busy work schedules, and family obligations, and somehow carved a path to completion—even if the final product did not turn out the way they had planned, nor happen as soon.

This is what I found: just as each person's creative project was personal and unique, so was their way of working on it. And that was true for me, too.

In talking to these people and analyzing my own experience, I also came to appreciate the value of constraints. Each person who works on a Big Thing experiences limits that can be accepted and also harnessed. Even if the limits seem to be negative, they can be transformed into something positive.

As I embarked on a journey to complete my own Big Thing, I started with the basics: my own physical being. I took lessons in posture, breathing, and meditation to create a sense of inner expansiveness, to ward off anxiety, and to become aware of a Big Thing as an experience in time. I also gave my sleeping and dreaming life its mysterious due.

As I learned about these things, I discovered that working on a big creative project is as much about *not* doing as about doing. You need to give your Big Thing, and yourself, a break throughout the process—both literally and figuratively. That break could be temporal and end up lasting for decades, as it did for me because my chronological age had not yet aligned with my purpose. Or it could be psychological in that you need to forgive yourself for stopping and know that you can always return. Or the break could be permanent because your reasons for wanting to do this thing were misplaced.

What's crucial is that you must, in the main, love doing this thing for its own sake—not for some external reward you may or may not receive because of it. Yes, the experience of working on it will be hard and unpleasant at times, but because the rewards are mainly intrinsic, it is worth doing. In a similar way that we love and commit to another person, despite rough spots in the relationship, we love and commit to a Big Thing.

The process of researching and writing this book felt very rough and halting. I constantly avoided trading the idealized version in my mind for the imperfect reality that required actual work. I needed the help and encouragement of others to make it to the finish, and learned that most people need help, and sometimes full-scale collaboration, to complete their projects too.

I do have some encouragement to offer readers, but I don't intend to be some kind of self-help guru and give a bunch of pep talks. I believe in the power of negative thinking. Once I decided to proceed with my own project I came to accept that I have terrible habits. I procrastinate, I'm lazy (although others would disagree), and I have low energy unless I'm under the gun. I put myself down and discount what I have accomplished. You will be right there with me as I deal with—and laugh over—all these flaws on the way to finishing my own Big Thing, this book.

ONE

The Value of the Long Arc

What's your *Big Thing* and why haven't you done it?

It could be a book or a script. A painting or a musical work. A new product, a startup company, or a charity. Whatever it is, it's a big creative idea of your own devising. But you work on it only fitfully, or you never even start, and the gap between aspiration and completion results in a psychic overhang that is uncomfortable to live with.

Do a little reconnaissance and you will find that many people have a Big Thing lurking in their psyches. A friend of mine wants to write a memoir about growing up as the daughter of a professional wrestler, but she is raising two children, and has a full-time job and no extra time. A composer friend has been trying to finish a musical for the last twenty years, but he's not satisfied with what he's done on his own and has been unable to find the right collaborator. A bartender in my neighborhood has been working on a note-taking app for people with attention deficit disorder, but his own case of ADHD keeps him from finishing it.

For these people, it's not enough to do work for others. They feel a deep-rooted need to create something of their own.

Big Things are many and varied, but they share these main qualities:

- They are personally meaningful to the people who seek to complete them.
- There is often no firm deadline for completing them.
- Their structure is large, complex, and at first unclear.
- They require sustained concentration and effort.

Before you embark on a Big Thing, it is important to look inside yourself and understand your main motivation. Be honest: Is your primary goal to become rich and famous, or a saint? Maybe you have been indulging in pleasant fantasies to that effect.

Motives can be mysterious, and mixed. Yes, your acclaim-seeking ego may be one driver of your goal. And that's not all bad. Narcissism gets a lot done in this world.

But here is one of many paradoxes that surround the Big Thing: ego may also be holding you back—and it may be the ultimate in narcissism *not* to do your Big Thing. Because when you don't do it, it can remain vague and perfect in your mind and allow you to nestle in the illusion of your greatness. Once you buckle down and try to do it, you are confronted with uncertainty and imperfection at every turn. It's hard! And your efforts are so paltry compared to how they appeared in your overinflated imaginings. In the end, then, committing to labor over the thing is less egotistical than continuing not to do it, since you are forced into a state of humility in the face of its—and your—flaws.

Good point, says the fearful part of yourself that is great at coming up with reasons not to do something: Isn't it folly to work on this thing that is the puny product of a limited mind—and that owing to its very magnitude carries a high chance of failure?

Not at all. I am going to argue that for some of us (not all of us) working on a Big Thing is one of the best ways to connect with the world. It is how some of us become most truly human.

Nancy Molitor, a psychotherapist practicing in Chicago, says many of her patients come to her not because of some outright calamity but because of an unmet creative need that is making them uneasy. Even if they say they are in therapy because of a problem in their work or family life, the discussion often comes around to some big dream never pursued. A woman with adult children may have wanted to get a Ph.D. or write a novel when she was twenty-five, but then marriage and children took precedence. A divorce or other life change can bring that yearning back to the fore.

Molitor sometimes treats people who are in their fifties, sixties, seventies, or beyond who never pursued their big projects and are now feeling deep regret about it. Usually, she said, she tells them it is not too late.

"We all want to leave something behind," she said. "We all want some part of ourselves to be remembered. Some people will say that's their children." But children may not be enough, especially after they grow up and pursue their own lives.

Suppose someone *is* facing a calamity—a health problem or a serious family issue. This can cause people to focus excessively on themselves and lose their perspective, Molitor said, in which case a big project can be a boon. "When you're working on something outside of yourself, it makes you feel more alive because you're seeing something concrete happening," she said. "It makes you feel more connected to the world and you have a reason to keep going. Also, it gives you structure."

As humans, we are built to maintain homeostasis in our physiological functions, said Molitor. Homeostasis reinforces stability, which can be achieved through structure. The same is true for our emotional well-being. A long-term project, stabilized by a structure, keeps our minds and our bodies running smoothly.

There's a reason that people who retire often don't do well—it's because they've suddenly lost their sense of structure. Just at the time in their lives that they have ample time to pursue their dream, they are at sea. Reestablishing the structure that their job gave them is a mighty task; it must be imposed from the inside rather than outside.

Sometimes people end up in Molitor's office because they experience a rejection of their Big Thing—say, a publisher turns down a book proposal or a startup fails to attract investors. In that case, they're letting other people determine the value of their project—a sign that it may be motivated mainly by narcissism. It's a delicate psychological balance. "You have to believe in yourself, but you can't take yourself so seriously that you live or die by the rejection or the acceptance," she said.

Reaching the state of equilibrium that Molitor describes is deeply fulfilling, but it is very hard to get to that point, whatever your age. You must leap over a kind of psychic abyss.

The influential twentieth-century psychologist Rollo May understood that individual acts of creation can help people realize their full potential and, through their impact, expand human consciousness. But in order to reach that stage, people must confront their own limits along with the doubts that arise from those limits—and make a commitment to proceed anyway.

People's own self-doubt, their friends and family, their other commitments, and society itself can erect barriers to this kind of creation. In *Man's Search for Himself*, first published in 1953, May noted that a numbing pressure to conform to societal norms, leading to a widespread feeling of emptiness, was preventing more people from expressing themselves creatively. A few years later the deadening aspects of the decade were immortalized in Sloan Wilson's *The Man in the Gray Flannel Suit*, whose main character loses his sense of identity as he tries to toe the corporate line in a meaningless PR job.

Many in "the Silent Generation" of the 1950s bowed to the conventions of the time and kept their expressions of individuality within a limited, acceptable range. Our era has taken on a different tenor. Individualism is almost fetishized now, although on a superficial level. In some circles there is almost too much pressure to come up with something new. Short-term creativity can even become a way to bypass hard work. The original things that seem to be valued most are bright and brief and viral.

May makes a distinction between "art as artificiality (as in 'artifice' or 'artful') and genuine art." All the showy artifice of our age conceals a shortage of true originality, and a pressure to adhere to the norms of the era as strong as it was in the fifties, though it takes a different form. All of our online bandwagons of approval-showing are a modern-day reflection of the universal human need for acceptance—which taken too far can obstruct the idiosyncratic honesty required to create something lasting.

Today we are pressured by social media to present an artificial self, in the form of posts and tweets, YouTube videos, and Instagrams. Some people mold and remold their online selves, the better to receive likes and thumbs-up, tweets, and other forms of approval. People also use their creative energies to promote themselves on the Internet, as a means to boost their careers and their "brand." That's another form of artifice. A cult of celebrity has furthered this fetishization of the self, as ordinary people seek to emulate the types of tweets and Instagram photos that generate millions of likes and followers.

In this way, people begin to equate popularity with value and meaning. Millions of views and clicks may well generate profit for some advertiser or media company, but it doesn't follow that the content is meaningful. Often quite the opposite.

These kinds of posts are not your deepest self, unless you are the most superficial of people. In fact, constant posting and liking and finding the best angle for your social media photo may actually obscure your true self. The problem of our time is that we are lured into these small, self-glorified, acceptance-seeking creations at the expense of deeper experiences. You could almost say that the outside world is conspiring to subvert deeper meaning.

As readers and consumers we can't help but be attracted to these promotional blips and pings. Reading and responding to books, and even watching movies, can be a way to react against this tendency. This is one reason that novels will not be going away anytime soon, doomsayers to the contrary. The mind craves the long arc that a book provides.

But an even more meaningful antidote to the problem is to create something with a long arc yourself—to evolve from receiver to producer. If it is something you believe in, it is not a sign of narcissism. It is how you express your truest being. It can be a way to make a meaningful contribution to the world and even leave a legacy.

To finish a Big Thing you must complete a series of much smaller things. But these smaller pieces are all related and connected to a larger whole that you have created. How can this not be good for a mind that confronts a daily dose of disparate tweets, Facebook posts, cat videos, overheard conversations, and news items from all over? Even at work, where we labor under the unifying structure of the organization, we are called upon to perform many different tasks, and multitasking is revered.

We need to place more value on *unitasking*: working steadily toward the creation of one thing. Unitasking is more important than ever in our spliced-up world. By forcing us to concentrate on one thing, it creates a structure inside our brain and provides structure in our daily lives. We may sometimes receive a big assignment at work that fulfills this role, but a project can be even more meaningful when it has sprung from our own minds, and is shaped by our own unique talents and values.

As I mentioned in my introduction, my Big Thing is this book. I am in my fifties and childless, and once I hit fifty my mortality loomed over me as never before. I needed to find a way to control my laziness before I died and left nothing behind except a few ephemeral newspaper articles. I made a commitment to write this book, for real this time.

But as I tried to work on my Big Thing, it was so easy to become distracted. I kept wanting to check Facebook and Twitter and my text messages and the news sites. This is a normal human tendency, according to Earl Miller, a neuroscientist at the Picower Institute for Learning and Memory at the Massachusetts Institute of Technology, and it becomes worse as we age and our cognitive capacity declines.

When we were evolving as primates, a little bit of information out there in the wilderness or the savanna was extremely important, he explained. It might be a tiger or some other animal leaping out at us. Our brains haven't evolved to keep up in the kind of environment we have now with all its technological distractions. "We can't adapt to it as quickly as we invented it," Miller said. "The brain is constantly craving that informational tap on the shoulder."

I asked him: What's actually happening in my brain when I get distracted, and freeze up, and procrastinate?

That's a deep question that scientists can't yet fully answer, Miller said, but they have been able to identify two general modes of brain processing: bottom up and top down. Bottom up is the raw sensory information coming into our brains. Top down is the knowledge we bring to a situation—what we need to ignore in order to achieve our goals. The prefrontal cortex is at the top of top-down processing. It tries to keep your eyes on the prize by filtering out distractions. Someone whose prefrontal cortex is strong is better at inhibiting stimuli—by shutting off neurons not related to a big goal.

When a person's prefrontal cortex is damaged they can no longer work toward long-term goals. "They become slaves to whatever stimulus is in the environment," he said. "They seem to lose the brakes on their brain that allow them to avoid distractions and engage in goal-directed behavior." The prefrontal cortex provides us with information about what possible goals might be out there, short and long term, and also helps us put together plans to achieve those goals.

"Do some people have brains that are naturally better at doing that?" I asked.

"Yes," Miller said.

"That's not fair."

"I know."

It's true you're going to have some natural disposition to be a focused person, but the brain is like a muscle, he said: The more you use it, the stronger it gets. "Neurons that don't fire together weaken their connections. Working on a long-term project will strengthen those pathways."

So if you seek to be a goal-oriented person who can accomplish large projects, then by all means you should practice doing that, or maybe start with smaller projects until you can handle a larger one, he said. And do your best to avoid distractions like email and Facebook while doing so, he added.

"For some reason, you only can activate a very small number of thoughts simultaneously in your brain," Miller said. All the knowledge of your lifetime is there in storage, but you can only activate one or two thoughts—or at most four—at a time. Unrelated technological stimuli will reduce the amount of related knowledge that you can extract at once.

This is possibly one of the worst times in history to get a Big Thing done. Our modern, sped-up, self-promoting lives, constantly interrupted by technology, have made it so. Not only that, but if you need to do research on your thing, it's so easy to google what you are trying to do and discover that someone else has already done it, or go down a rabbit hole of possible sources and materials and related links until you are presented with a seeming infinity of possible ways to proceed with your thing. How do you narrow it all down? How do you find the best way to proceed?

One woman I talked to who struggled for years to finish her dissertation said she felt as if she would have to read all the books in the library before she could finish her paper. She admitted that she was prey to that great enemy of completion: perfectionism.

When you set out to create something, you can become paralyzed by the possibilities in front of you. At a certain point you have to accept that you can't read every book in the library, or check each of 1,454,673 Google results, and work with what you have.

We need to give ourselves a break for failing to complete our big projects. But we also need to recognize that the excuses we make for failing to create our Big Things could be disguising a basic fear—one that has existed since the beginning of humankind: that our Big Thing will be a failure.

But will it be a failure by whose measure and whose standards? According to you? According to critics? Even if it turns out to be terrible, or have no impact (according to some subjective/objective standard), was it still worth it to do it? Yes, if you felt a compulsion to do it and it was hanging over you, and when you finished it that over-hang was gone. Even if you decide that on balance it was a failure, the experience could help you chart a different course the next time.

Overcoming a fear of failure requires immense courage. As the Danish philosopher Søren Kierkegaard wrote, the inevitable result of passing over from a state of possibility into one of actuality is a sense of anxiety. In this intermediate state, self-doubt and fear are necessary. Creativity, Kierkegaard writes, involves reconciling opposites: the infinity of the universe on the one hand and the spec-ificity and limits of the individual self on the other. Into that breach rushes anxiety, until the self can find a footing and begin to create a structure inside the emptiness.

This is why making a commitment to the Big Thing is impera-tive. You may need to do it publicly and enlist others around you to hold you accountable. I will describe efforts along those lines in other chapters. Commitment, aided by willpower and habit, is just about the only force powerful enough to fight the extreme desire to flee the ambiguity of the creative state.

So suppose you have been telling yourself, over and over, I must do my Big Thing. My life won't be meaningful unless I do it. But many of us don't take the next steps because of the lure and power of procrastination. This is not the same kind of procrastination that surrounds some task like housecleaning, which you avoid because it is repetitive and tedious. Here you avoid it because you don't know how to proceed, and the work is connected to your deepest identity. So you rely on your future self to get the work done.

My present self has a tendency to ask: Why must you create? Why can't you just be? When I actively avoid working on my Big Thing, food tastes better and movies on the Lifetime channel seem unusually compelling.

Christine Tappolet, a philosophy professor at the University of Montreal, has said that procrastination reflects a lack of concern for our future selves, to the point that we are willing to harm them in favor of our present selves. She writes: "Future selves are considered to be strangers, to whom one can pass the buck and impose a heavy and uncompensated burden."

As a way to combat this tendency, Tappolet proposes working actively to empathize with the fate of one's future selves. This idea appeals to me. I should look at my future selves as coworkers I don't want to let down. In my day job, I am rarely lazy, because I have colleagues and supervisors to whom I am accountable. Even beyond the fact that in order to receive my paycheck I must complete my assignments, I don't want to let my colleagues down as people. I care too much about what they think of me. If I treated my work colleagues the way I treat my future selves, I would soon be fired for not doing my job. Why not give myself at least the same consideration I give others?

If you are employed, the organization where you work depends on a division of labor. Managers delegate work to employees, who each carry out tasks in service of a whole. It comforts me to think of my Big Thing as both a literal and metaphorical division of labor. Literally, in order to write this chapter, I have divided a somewhat arbitrary estimated length, 8,000 words, by the number of days I have allotted myself to write it, 28, and come up with 286 words a day. That doesn't seem so daunting!

This helps me turn the "future self" idea of procrastination on its head. I imagine delegating the labor of this chapter to twenty-eight future selves, each of whom will perform her allotted task. Except that the organization that these selves are working for is not a company, but my own truest self, working bit by bit to achieve her truest potential.

And just as I said, this is really hard! Everything I wrote above is turning out to be true. My writing about the struggle to complete the Big Thing is nowhere near as good as I imagined it would be. There are deep, important, and complex ideas that I cannot find a way to express, and even if I can, I don't know where to put them. I'm writing the paragraphs of this chapter piecemeal with no idea how they will all fit together. I am panicking right now. My stomach is alternately tied up in knots and doing flips. I am hanging on to arithmetic (just 286 words today! that's all!) as though for dear life.

And now I understand why I was so lazy for all those years. It was a way to forestall this anxiety I am now feeling on a daily basis.

I have long berated myself for being lazy when it comes to my personal aspirations. I consider myself possessed of "a fine natural indolence," as Virginia Woolf describes the heroine in *The Voyage Out*.

Looking through the scholarly and medical literature, I see lots of research on anxiety but very little on laziness. Think about it: What kind of tangible symptom does laziness produce? A sense of sluggishness maybe, of being slow on the uptake.

By contrast, just look at these symptoms associated with anxiety, from the medical site WebMD.

Sudden overwhelming fear
Palpitations
Sweating
Trembling
Shortness of breath
Sense of choking
Chest pain
Nausea
Dizziness
A feeling of being detached from the world (de-realization)
Fear of dying
Numbness or tingling in the limbs or entire body
Chills or hot flushes

It's true that laziness can correlate with depression. And if you are lazy in all respects, in both your mind and your body, you could end up being obese and develop diseases because of that. But laziness doesn't send you in desperation to your GP the way the above symptoms can.

And in fact, I went running to my own GP while writing this chapter. As I struggled to establish new habits while creating something out of nothing, and having doubts about the whole enterprise, I started having stomach pains almost every day. It reminded me of when I first moved to New York and wondered if I could handle living in the big city and whether I really was good enough to work at the *New York Times*.

I was hoping my doctor would prescribe me the medicine I had taken briefly back then—Klonopin—but she refused because, she said, it is addictive. I was disappointed. I had been hoping for a fun, addictive drug. Instead I left with a prescription for something called Atarax.

"Just out of curiosity, does anyone ever come and see you for laziness?" I asked my doctor as I was leaving. She seemed puzzled by the question. After a pause she said: "Sometimes people ask for a doctor's slip when they don't want to go in to work or to school." In effect she was saying that some patients are lazy and want to *continue* being lazy. The idea of someone coming in wanting to be cured of their laziness was foreign to her. I guess you go straight to the psychologist for that one.

I realize that *laziness* and *anxiety* are not really congruent terms. Anxiety is more clearly a condition and a diagnosis. Calling yourself lazy is more of a value judgment.

Nancy Molitor certainly thinks it is. People continually tell themselves that they're lazy, or stupid, or a screwup, or even an all-out loser, and they're held back by these negative statements that they make about themselves, she said. Often (not always) we heard these messages during our childhood, and they took root and never left:

"You forget even who said it, but you accept it as reality, and you turn it on yourself."

A Big Thing has the potential to augment those self-criticisms. The anxiety that inevitably accompanies creation could harm your mental and your physical health. Working on your project could also negatively affect your home life and your day job.

Often working on a Big Thing means pursuing meaning over happiness, at least temporarily. Yes, happiness and meaningfulness can overlap, but not always. According to the results of a large survey published in the *Journal of Positive Psychology*, "concerns with personal identity and expressing the self contributed to meaning but not happiness." In addition, "higher levels of worry, stress and anxiety were linked to higher meaningfulness but lower happiness." And happiness "is largely present oriented, whereas meaningfulness involves integrating past, present and future."

So which is it to be: happiness or meaning? I don't place any value judgment on choosing happiness. But I do think some people have that inner pull to pursue meaning, and if they don't, laziness and guilt set in, which leads to a slow, cumulative regret over the course of their lives—different and ultimately more costly than the unhappiness they would have felt if they had pursued their deep goal.

There is a reward for working through the unhappiness and anxiety. Once you have made your Big Thing part of the structure of your life, you can experience the homeostasis that helps you become more stable. Moreover, this is a structure that contains deep, personal meaning.

Once you have made it over to the other side, anxiety recedes and you achieve a state of full concentration. All the distractions and fripperies of the Internet are gone from your mind; worries and ruminations about your personal faults and problems are swept aside as the light of your mind focuses on this and this alone.

It is then that one can experience the joy of creation. Rollo May uses the word *joy* in contrast to happiness or pleasure. "The artist, at the moment of creating, does not experience gratification or satisfaction," he writes, but rather "joy defined as the emotion that goes with heightened consciousness, the mood that accompanies the experiencing of actualizing one's own potentialities." More recently the psychologist Mihaly Csikszentmihalyi has referred to this as a state of flow.

I am just beginning this journey, but there is one thing I have already learned: the hardest part is to start. The project is at its most amorphous at the very beginning, and the more vague it is the more anxiety it causes. Not only that, but your habits are not in place to work on this big blob of an amorphous mess.

It took me until the age of fifty-three to start writing a nonfiction book, as I placed all manner of fears and excuses and distractions between a book and myself.

Once I finally made the commitment to this Big Thing, working on it has been a wrenching, painful affair—less so as the days go by but still difficult. But once I sit down and begin writing, it is not so hard. I wish I could remember this.

Goethe, in *Faust,* described this battle well as a struggle between repose and exertion:

Two souls abide, alas, within my breast,
And each one seeks for riddance from the other.

The moment when you heave yourself over from inactivity to activity is the hardest to endure. It is the place where unproductive thoughts and delaying tactics are most likely to enter.

Getting out of bed to start writing reminded me of Zeno's Paradox. In order to get to my desk I had to cross half the distance from my bedroom to the living room, and then half of that distance, and half of that distance, and so on. Therefore it was impossible to get there.

This is where the principle of inertia comes into play. In physics, inertia is defined as "the tendency of an object in motion to remain in motion, or an object at rest to remain at rest, unless acted upon by a force." When we apply the word *inertia* more loosely to human beings, we think of it as a state of sluggishness, but it is also the case that once we (the objects) start moving, we are likely to continue moving—up to a point, anyway.

We keep doing work at the office through the process of inertia. If we stop to rest (and as living beings we do need breaks), a force known as our managers and coworkers acts upon us to start again.

But when it is just us, with our personal creative projects that no one else really cares about, what is the force that can act upon us to start? It must be our own will, which, if we keep exercising it for a period of time, is supposed to turn magically into a habit.

There was one small change I made in my life to force myself to start writing this book. I love and crave coffee and must have a cup in the morning. Previously I always had my first cup of coffee in bed, usually while reading a Scandinavian mystery. Once I knew I had to write this book, I forced myself to have my coffee at my desk and to start writing.

After years of morning laziness before leaving for my day job, I managed to make this an ironclad rule. Well, there's been some backsliding. Some mornings, I manage to convince myself I don't even want coffee—that's how strong my resistance is to working on this thing. But overall, I succeeded in setting up a trigger, the coffee, to set my work in motion.

I found that actually saying, "The hardest part is to start" out loud was helpful. It had an incantatory quality that helped get me on my feet.

To keep myself on track, I also started small. When embarking on a Big Thing, there is a tendency to want to start big, by devoting long hours to it and shunting other parts of your life aside. It's understandable to want to make up for lost time this way, but in general that's a bad idea.

And I also didn't try to accomplish any other big goals, like losing weight or cleaning out all my closets. As Roy Baumeister and John Tierney write in their book, *Willpower*, "You have a finite amount of willpower that becomes depleted as you use it." Also: "You use the same stock of willpower for all manner of tasks."

"When people have to make a big change in their lives, their efforts are undermined if they are trying to make other changes as well," they write.

I suspect I have even less energy than most people, and I knew I needed to use my willpower strategically. And so when I began my little requirement of drinking my first cup of coffee at my desk, I attached a very modest stipulation to this new behavior. I merely had to write one-half page on a topic related to my book or my struggles writing it. That was all.

That is all I did for the first full month of working on my book, except for a few days of backsliding, mentioned above, and one day when I had a hangover.

After the month was over, I began to work in earnest on the first chapter (which is this chapter). It was helpful to clarify what I was attempting to do in the half page of the notebook. Then I moved on to my draft of the first chapter, and in that way I slowly increased my daily output.

By simply forcing myself to start working each day with very little in the way of requirements, I created the environment for inertia to move its energy in the opposite direction of resting. And sure enough, once I got going, I kept going for a while, often even exceeding my quota.

The groundbreaking American psychologist William James (1842–1910) recognized that forming a habit is first of all "a chapter in physics rather than physiology or psychology." The nervous organs, he said in his famous essay on habit, can easily be launched on a "false career" because of inertia.

How does one turn that powerful force in the opposite direction, toward constructive action? By deciding to "launch ourselves with as strong and decided an initiative as possible" toward a new way of behaving. James himself knew how hard this was to do: he suffered through severe depression and self-doubt before he came out the other side and began writing his masterpieces, including *The Principles of Psychology*, of which his essay on habit is one chapter.

Also from experience, James knew that "a sharp period of suffering" may be necessary to redirect the force of inertia. I feel that suffering each morning before I force myself to get up and write. Knowing that it will ease (at least for a while) once I get to my desk and start writing helps force me to get up. In the beginning stages, "Never suffer an exception to occur," James admonishes. It is during this vulnerable period that the brain must be given the opportunity to form a new groove for a new habit.

Recent neuroscience has confirmed many of James's theories on habit. As the author Charles Duhigg has explained, the behavior surrounding habitual activity is stored in the brain's basal ganglia, which cause that succession of actions to become automatic. The brain, ever on the lookout to save effort, can then focus its attention on other tasks—such as the higher-level mental work required to get a Big Thing done.

After a few months of working on this book, I still experience the suffering of working on it, although it has lessened somewhat. I know that in some ways my age is working against me. I no longer have the plasticity of youth that makes the formation of habits much easier. "READ!" I wrote twenty-five years ago on the essay on habit where James notes that someone's character has "set like plaster and will never soften again" by the age of thirty. Why didn't I try harder back then to develop good habits?

I have, however, made a commitment. Ongoing commitment is a key feature of a Big Thing, just as it is in a marriage. Once you commit to it, even when you aren't working on it, your unconscious brain is picking at it behind the scenes. As many artists and scientists have attested, this can cause creative breakthroughs to occur at the most unexpected moments—while one is in the shower or in a car or on the subway or walking down the street, for example.

Revelations like these seem to come out of nowhere, but that's not really the case. The unconscious has been working and worrying on the project all along. But the breakthrough would never have been possible without the initial commitment of the conscious mind.

Sometimes "laziness" is not avoidance but rather a call to stop working and take a necessary break. A creator of a Big Thing needs to discern the difference between "good" lazy and "evil" lazy.

"Evil" lazy is a kind of cowardice. Rollo May lays on the guilt trip pretty thick: "If you do not express your own original ideas," he intones, "if you do not listen to your own being, you will have betrayed yourself. Also you will have betrayed our community in failing to make your contribution to the whole."

"Good" lazy is the result of an exquisite understanding of the needs of your body and mind. It happens when you know that your body and mind need a rest. As May puts it, "It might be that the conscious work has been more fruitful because it has been interrupted and the rest has given back to the mind its force and freshness."

And so I will stop writing now and take a rest. But is this "good" lazy or "evil" lazy? I have so much more work to do before I can know for sure.

TWO

Mind and Body

So *many of us* live in our heads, rushing toward a future that never arrives. Just look at the people around you, bending their heads forward as if outsourcing their mental energy onto their smartphones and computers. These days it can be so easy to forget that your head is connected to a body. We are losing our creative ballast as we project it onto our devices. That's another reason it's so hard to work on a big project. We often lack a center of physical gravity from which to create a thing of substance.

Before starting this chapter, I paused to consider my physical state. My shoulders were hunched, my back was tight, I was breathing shallowly. I was worried about all the things I had to do that day, and my body reflected that. Trying to unscrunch myself, I thought: Wouldn't the quality of my work be higher if my body were more relaxed? And yet it was so hard to relax for any length of time.

Maybe, I thought, I need to treat my body more like a machine that must be tended and regulated. Out of regular physical maintenance, superior mental performance can spring.

Listen to your body, we are told. I have not done that nearly enough in my life. Now I am really trying to listen, but sometimes it's hard to tell, exactly, what the message is.

To get my body into better condition for the long haul of a Big Thing, I thought it would be smart to concentrate on the physiological basics, like breathing, posture, and movement. Recognizing that my disembodied state was too far advanced for me to cure on my own, I consulted experts in all three areas. Talking to them, I came to realize two things that have a Zen-like, paradoxical quality: To do is to undo. And to do is to not do.

To release new ideas, and to develop the physical and mental endurance to pursue a Big Thing, we may need to undo unhealthy physical habits that have developed over a lifetime and that are now so ingrained that we are unconscious of them. And once we finally commit ourselves to working on our Big Thing day after day, we must not let the sheer bigness of it frighten us into working on it nonstop. Our body needs us to take breaks from it.

In some ways, my experts ended up giving me lessons in the obvious. But it's amazing how living in the modern world can distance you from the most obvious things—such as the fact that the body affects what the mind does, and vice versa.

Through the way we breathe and hold ourselves and move, we can restrict our potential, in both literal and metaphorical ways. By returning to a more natural way of physical being—the kind we were born with—we can achieve an expansiveness that lives in the moment and lends itself to sustained creativity.

I started with my breathing, because what is more basic to life than breath? It is the internal measure of our lives. It stands to reason that if you aren't breathing properly, not enough oxygen is going to your brain, which will inhibit your ability to think clearly and creatively. With that in mind, I decided to take a breathing class from Belisa Vranich, a clinical psychologist who believes that people are suffocating from their own stress.

Vranich's studio is in the Flatiron District of Manhattan, in that particularly confusing part of town where the angle of Broadway makes it hard to tell east from west. Sirens wailed loudly outside during the first few minutes of our conversation, and so I was in a fine state of stress when we began.

Vranich could pass for a California surfer. She projects warmth, kindness, and confidence, and she has rock-hard abs. She wanted to establish a baseline before she worked on improving my breathing, so she took out a measuring tape and had me take a deep breath.

Then she told me to hold my breath for as long as possible without passing out.

First, she said, I'm a vertical breather: on the inhale I become taller and on the exhale I come down. That's a very popular type of breath, she said, but it's not very efficient.

Then she used the measuring tape to determine my vital lung capacity, which is the difference between your inhale and your exhale, and is a good indicator of longevity. "Your inhale is thirty-six and unfortunately your exhale is also thirty-six," she told me. "You actually don't have a difference between either number. I've only seen this twice before. I'm so sorry." People with bad vital lung capacity also have a higher risk of incontinence, it turns out.

On the bright side, my breath hold—an indicator of the balance of oxygen and carbon dioxide in my body—was 51, which is higher than average. Apparently the combination of my numbers showed that I am able to tolerate a high amount of discomfort. But I am not using my anatomy in the way that it was meant to be used.

My two-hour breathing lesson cost $350. I felt a little silly paying that much money for something that babies know how to do without any classes at all. But that's just the point, Vranich said. Until the age of five, most of us are breathing the way we are meant to breathe, pushing our bellies out on the inhale and pulling them in on the exhale. Then various terrible and stressful things happen to us as we get older, and we start breathing the "wrong" way.

"Where's the biggest part of your lungs?" she asked as we sat together on the floor. In answer she pulled up her shirt and gave her abdomen three big slaps that echoed throughout the room. Am I using that part of my lungs when I breathe vertically? No. I am mainly using the tiny nubs of my shoulders to breathe, and *there are no lungs there.*

"Your neck and shoulders were never meant to be breathing muscles," Vranich said. It sounded so obvious when she put it that way. A lot of people think their back and shoulder pain has to do with working long hours on the computer. More likely, she said, it's because thousands of times a day and millions of times a year, they're using their neck and shoulder muscles to breathe instead of their bellies.

Most of the fatigue people feel is related to the body not getting enough oxygen, Vranich asserted. It's the breath from the lower part of your lungs that brings more oxygen to your brain. Oxygen is cell fuel, including for your brain cells. If you breathe from your abdomen, that leads to better productivity and creativity—and, with a big project, more endurance. "All our senses are being dulled by the fact that we don't have enough oxygen in our bodies," she said.

Over and over in the Flatiron studio, we practiced what she said was the right way to breathe—to expand outward on the inhale and squeeze in on the exhale.

"Your body is built to breathe this way," she assured me, but although I had apparently done this naturally as a baby, it was now extremely counterintuitive. My shoulders kept scrunching up as I could feel myself failing to follow the instructions. "Don't worry about your shoulders right now!" she said.

"Think about all the real estate in your body that you haven't been using," she said, as my head began to tingle from all the unaccustomed oxygen it was receiving while I used my abdomen to breathe horizontally. An image came to me of a row of empty mansions filled with gorgeous rooms and furniture, and no one living in them.

Then I had a dismaying thought. Maybe I'm not inherently a low-energy person. Maybe I have low energy because I've been breathing incorrectly for decades, and if only I had done it the right way all along I could have developed more stamina to create a multitude of Big Things.

When you use your abdomen to breathe, you make use of the diaphragm, a dome-shaped muscle the size of a small pizza that is attached to your bottom rib. On the inhale it's designed to flatten out and push your ribs open. On the exhale it curls up and enables your whole body to squeeze air out. Your exhale is extremely important, because it gets all the stale air out of your body.

The diaphragm conveys air to your lungs with every breath (provided you use it), and at the same time it massages the lower part of your body, Vranich said. How happy does that make your liver, colon, and stomach? As a result, digestive problems like constipation, irritable bowel, and acid reflux tend to diminish when we practice better breathing, and we tend to sleep better, too. The fight-or-flight mechanism that accompanies shallow breaths is replaced by a natural state of resting and digesting.

Even the superfit Vranich looked pregnant as she leaned forward to demonstrate, in an exaggerated manner, the proper breathing technique. She made me pull down the elastic of my sweatpants and do it, too; my muffin top jiggled.

Nora Ephron felt bad about her neck. I feel bad about my stomach. When we have trouble owning and accepting parts of our bodies, we are unable to fully inhabit our physical space, and this constricts our thinking. This happens literally, in the sense that it contorts our muscles and bones so that we are out of alignment and cause ourselves pain. The twistedness of internal avoidance brings on shallow breathing that restricts the flow of oxygen to our brain. And it may cause us not to go certain places in our thoughts. (On the other hand, the twisted path can be quite complex and beautiful in its way, and more so for not being so simple and straightforward.)

Two inches below your belly button is the life force known as your chi and the seat of your intuition, Vranich said. It's why we say we have a gut feeling about something. Deep belly breaths have been linked to intuitive wisdom in Buddhism, Taoism, and other religions.

That got me wondering: What was I failing to perceive by wanting to disown this part of myself?

*   *   *

I knew that as I was disowning parts of my body, like my stomach, I was overusing others, like my neck, shoulders, and back, causing me to feel off-kilter and tense. To feel more comfortable in my own body while working on my Big Thing, I decided to take posture lessons.

To create something new, I realized, I would need to perform certain actions, like typing, over and over again. It would be wise for me to consider my physical position as I did so. Repetitive movements, if done incorrectly, could cause discomfort and injury.

Initially I had looked at the posture lessons as a preventive health measure. But once I started taking them I realized that good posture literally opens you up to heightened creativity by reconnecting your head to your body.

"Imagine the top of your head," said my posture teacher, Lindsay Newitter, during my first lesson. "Don't do anything, just imagine it." It was surprisingly effective. Even though my head was seemingly not moving during the exercise, the act of imagining it changed things for the better.

Newitter is a practitioner of the Alexander Technique, which is all about understanding and correcting the misuse of tension. Frederick Matthias Alexander, who developed the technique in the early twentieth century, was an actor who developed a chronic case of hoarseness that threatened to end his career. After consulting doctors to no avail, he came up with his technique through trial and error, by watching himself in the mirror and becoming aware of unconscious physical habits—like pulling his head and back down into his spine while depressing his larynx—that were placing unnecessary strain on his voice. He came to realize that people unknowingly place undue stress on their bodies in many ways, causing aches, pains, and illness. Creators of Big Things including George Bernard Shaw and Aldous Huxley consulted Alexander when their pain became so intense that they could no longer work regularly.

Alexander understood that people don't perceive themselves

correctly, causing them to move in unnatural ways. This is why he advised enlisting a teacher to gently correct one's misalignments. Indeed, after Newitter corrected my posture while I was standing I felt as if I were pitched forward until I saw in the mirror that I was quite straight.

We think of the neck as connecting to our head at the shoulders when actually the hinge is near our earlobes, Newitter said. And our hip joints are lower than we think, closer to the pelvis. These misperceptions cause our image and our expression of ourselves to be compressed. This, I considered, is also true psychologically. People so often place limits on what they think they can do in life. And it can show in the way they hold themselves—an inner and outer reality that meet in a circle.

During my lessons, I came to understand that we get in our own way, both physically and mentally. There is a psychological equivalent to the unnecessary tension we place on our bodies. In fact, one feeds into the other, creating a vicious circle of tension. Life crushes you down and compresses you, and you need to use your imagination to counteract that, and move higher.

Once we release the tension that has collected in our bodies from a lifetime of stress, we can allow ourselves to lengthen and widen. From physical expansiveness, creativity can emerge. The Alexander Technique encourages us to see our body as an integrated whole rather than a collection of disparate parts. From a base of physical wholeness, a mental structure can become clearer.

Actors, ballet dancers, and other performers are much more attuned to their posture and breathing because the success of their work depends on the way others see them in the moment. Writers and artists, who often labor alone, don't have the same incentive to position themselves correctly.

Echoing Belisa Vranich, Newitter said that most young children naturally have healthy posture. Then life's stresses and indignities begin to push and prod their way into their very bones. Sometimes people become very emotional during posture lessons, as they remember an event from their childhood that they now realize corresponds to an unhealthy pose made permanent through habit, she said.

Newitter, in her midthirties, has the lithe build and gait of a ballet dancer. I was surprised to learn that she grew up with scoliosis; there was no evidence of it in her graceful frame. She wore a brace for five years when she was in her teens, so it did most of the work to hold her up. After it came off, she started taking acting classes at New York University and developed horrible postural habits that she knew she would have to correct if she was to be a convincing actress. When she started learning the Alexander Technique it was as if a light went on.

The name of Newitter's Manhattan company is the Posture Police, which brings to mind some kind of posture dominatrix. In fact, Newitter is an exceedingly gentle teacher, subtly using her hands to realign the body so it can move in the way it was designed to move.

"Natural posture is actually very comfortable," she said. "You can breathe easily and you shouldn't really feel like you're holding yourself up at all."

The posture class was subtle because it was not about doing but undoing. Newitter put her hands under various parts of my body and had me fall into them. At the end I walked around the room feeling as if I were in charm school.

The idea behind posture training is to create a neutral position from which your thinking and goals can flow. You can go inward for a while and journey purely in your thought space, but you don't have to live there, Newitter said. You can always return to your neutral physical position for balance.

When your posture is out of whack, your bones go out of alignment, creating a cascading effect all along your body, resulting in a kind of inner physical noise that makes it hard to concentrate.

I wondered: Isn't it possible to think creatively if you are hunched up all small? I think of plants that manage to grow inside tiny cracks on the sidewalk, or what about bonsai trees? Newitter acknowledged that beautiful work might flow from a tortured posture. But at least give yourself the option of learning a different way, she said. "It's not about having perfect posture. It's about having the choice to do whatever you want."

She advises spending at least ten minutes a day on what she calls constructive rest. That's where you lie in a semi-supine position (knees raised) and think about the work you plan to do. This causes gravity to exert itself on your back, and helps your spine decompress. "It helps you to release the things that are already there that you don't want to be holding."

"Allow the head to release out from the top of the spine," Newitter says on an audiotape she created for people to play during a session of continuous rest. "Allow the back of the head to lengthen and the front of the neck to lengthen. And it's just an allowing, not a pulling, tensing, or active doing." At home, guided by her voice, I gave myself mental directions along the rest of my body.

The first time I tried the continuous rest exercise, I felt like Alice in Wonderland after she ate cake with the sign that said EAT ME. My neck felt so long!

Many knowledge workers are disconnected from their bodies—until an unhealthy repetitive motion causes an injury, and then they become exquisitely aware of the connection in the form of pain, said Alan Hedge, an ergonomics professor at Cornell University.

The way you position yourself and move while you work has a major effect on your mental endurance and your ability to think clearly, he said. In particular, if a project is long and hard, you must incorporate regular breaks as you work.

Whether the effort is physical or mental, when people are working intensely they need to build in periods of recovery, Hedge said. Research shows that the ability to perform intense mental work drops after about twenty minutes. Be aware of this and take a break after twenty minutes—unless you are completely unaware of the time passing, and in a state of flow, in which case you won't be checking the time at all. Do something completely different for at least two or three minutes—take a walk or pace around or listen to music—and then go back to your project, he said.

Muscles have molecules inside them, called myoglobin, that provide you with oxygen, Hedge explained. After any intense activity, those molecules need to be recharged during a period of rest. The same principle is at work in the brain, except the brain is using glucose to think and create. When the glucose runs low—symptoms include forgetting what you just read or becoming easily distracted—it's time to take a break.

Before this book, I was taking what was in effect a decades-long break from my Big Thing. Now, when I take a break during the day, it's hard to tell whether I'm procrastinating or giving my brain a well-earned opportunity to recharge its glucose. How can I tell the difference?

During a needed break you tend to rest, Hedge said. When you procrastinate you tend to fill up the time with displacement activities— laundry, tidying, errands, answering emails, and so on. This, I later learned, is what researchers call "structured procrastination": it gives you a sense of progress and completion that a longer-term endeavor so seldom provides.

When your mind starts wandering, it's best to take a short stroll, or drink some tea, or listen to some relaxing music. After at least a few minutes of this your body will return to full efficiency, Hedge said.

Before I started writing this chapter I went away on vacation for a week and did not work on the book at all, taking long naps and reading mysteries instead. I felt guilty confessing this to Hedge, but his response was, "Good!" Actually, a short vacation from working is healthy for the body, he said, and he was sure my subconscious had been working on the book the whole time.

When I asked Hedge for advice on writing this book, he said it should come down to two things: baby steps and routine. Realize that a hundred words here and a hundred there will add up over time. And try to set up a regular time and place to write them.

I couldn't help thinking of Franz Kafka. Surely he was physically uncomfortable and erratic while writing such angst-ridden works as *The Metamorphosis*. But when I consulted Mason Currey's book, *Daily Rituals: How Artists Work*, I found that although Kafka lived in cramped, noisy quarters and frequently suffered from chest pain, twitching stomach muscles, and insomnia, he still exercised twice a day and took daily walks, plus he routinely wrote at least several hours a night after returning home from his day job before (trying) to go to sleep. So he both had a regular routine and suffered—those two things are not mutually exclusive.

Hedge made me realize that if you work on your Big Thing over a period of years, your ergonomic requirements may change. These changes are not necessarily linear, and they may or may not link up to your age. Hand and wrist pain can strike at any age. If you are in your forties your vision is likely to change much more rapidly than in any other decade, which could require a shift in the size of your screen and your font, and determine how far away you sit from your computer.

There are plenty of websites available, including one offered by Cornell University, to help you analyze your ergonomics. But as Alexander realized, it can be hard for people to see themselves as they really are. For about the cost of a plumber, you can bring someone in to analyze your situation, Hedge said.

Heeding his advice, I paid $120 to have Lindsay Newitter come to my apartment and look at my writing setup, and it was money well spent.

I do my writing while sitting in a wooden chair with a cushion on the seat. Right away Newitter could see that although the back of my chair was nice and straight, the seat angled down and away from my body too much. There was no need for a fancy office chair, she said, but she advised buying a basic wooden chair with a straight back and a straight seat for better positioning.

She also said that the table where I was working was too high for me, so we moved to a lower-down desk that I have in front of my living room window. She placed books under my feet and a pillow between my back and the chair so I was supported from back to front, and grounded from feet to head. Then she watched me type. If possible, she said, I might want to buy a wider keyboard to avoid scrunching into myself as I type.

The adjustments and suggestions she made were minimal, but they had the effect of making me feel more . . . three-dimensional.

We don't really live as if we possess three dimensions, Newitter said. Instead we have a very "front-centric" view of ourselves because that's where our eyes take us. All of our technology is literally pulling us away from ourselves, making us rush ahead unthinkingly instead of allowing us to occupy our own true space. That complex, idiosyncratic inner space needs to expand in order for a beautiful Big Thing to grow.

Writing a book is just as physical as running a marathon, Newitter maintained. In fact, sitting and typing day after day could end up being more of a strain than running. Whatever your big project is, if you're not in the present moment, it will be harder to do the work, and your body sets the stage for that.

Alexander talked about a concept known as "endgaining," where we get ahead of ourselves. In short, "You're there before you're there." When we move our bodies toward the future rather than the present, we tend to compress them, causing discomfort and making us feel smaller than we really are.

I have a tendency to forget to breathe when I am typing. Newitter urged me to slow down my typing speed sometimes (it's very fast) so I can relearn breathing while I think and type. "You can begin to associate breath and expansion with thinking," she said.

These small changes, I realized, would help me feel more like one whole piece. Instead of feeling fragmented and ahead of myself, I can feel integrated and in the moment, the better to create something new.

I like to write longhand in a notebook, and in our session we went over the best way to do that. She told me to avoid grasping the pen too tightly, and I did some lovely loop-de-loops to put me in a relaxed frame of mind before I did some actual writing. She took a picture of me while I was doing it because I looked so good.

Newitter also showed me the right and wrong way to use a mouse—right way, just use your finger. Wrong way, get the whole back of your hand and wrist involved; it's not necessary and can lead to pain down the line.

As I saw the back of her hand tense up during her "wrong" demonstration, an outline of a tendon rising to handle the stress, I realized that working on a Big Thing is all about efficiency, right down to our bones.

"I don't know if I can do this."

I was partway up Piestewa Peak in Arizona's Phoenix Mountains, breathing in gasps, sweat pouring down my face, and certain I was about to vomit. My guide was Jim Levine, a physician at the Mayo Clinic in Scottsdale and an expert on obesity prevention who believes that it is evil to sit too much and that humans are meant to be moving throughout the day.

As I prepared to write this chapter about the body's relationship to the Big Thing, I immediately thought of Levine, as I had interviewed him for a *Times* column on how the body needs breaks during the workday. Talking to him for my book, I found out that in addition to publishing two novels and two nonfiction books, he had also written a novella in Italian and was at work on a stage play. He did all this while holding down a full-time medical job, serving as a professor at Arizona State University, and codirecting an obesity prevention program there.

Of course I asked him what his secret was.

"Every day I climb the mountain," he answered during a phone interview, and at first I thought he was speaking metaphorically. But then he explained that he literally climbs Piestewa Peak first thing in the morning just about every day he is in Arizona. "It takes an hour and forty minutes," he told me. I proceeded to invite myself to Scottsdale to get a taste of that productive mountain air.

Once on the mountain, I realized that those were Jim minutes, not Phyllis minutes. About a half hour in, I sat panting on a rock, wondering whether to continue upward or admit defeat.

Levine had been bounding up the craggy rocks like a mountain goat, then waiting patiently and extending a hand when necessary as I struggled to find my footing. He'd been up and down this mountain around a thousand times; by now his muscle memory knew which rocks and crevices would propel him most efficiently. He didn't need to think about it the way I did.

Half the people on the mountain appeared to know Levine; it's where he conducts most of his social life. A brief hello, a few moments of heartfelt chat—it's the kind of interaction that suits him. As I sat there wheezing and nauseous on the rock, he had time to make a new friend: Richard, who like me needed a rest. Richard, as it turned out, had an apartment two floors below the one that Levine owns in the Hotel Valley Ho in Scottsdale.

After about ten minutes, my breath was fully caught and I felt ready to continue. "You see that metal railing up there?" Levine said as we set off. "It takes eleven minutes [Jim minutes, I feared] to get there, and then we're almost at the top."

We passed the railing, and soon we were nearly there. I saw the other people who had sweated their way to the top exulting on nearby rocks. "Now, we're going to go up the hard way, but I know you can do it," he said. I groaned as I looked at the steep rock face above me. One foot at a time, I made it to the top, where a medallion marked this as the very highest spot on the mountain.

We sat and took in the panoramic view of Scottsdale and Phoenix, cradled by mountains. Birds flew nearby and he delighted in the long whooshing noises they made. This is the best place to have a meeting, he said, because after the effort of the climb people seem to home in on what is truly important. And whether he is alone or with others, it's a healthy, natural way to start the day, without the distractions of technology. "Sometimes, if I've had a bad day, it's the only thing I achieve all day," he said.

Like me, Levine struggled the first time he climbed the mountain, but by now he'd learned the most efficient way up and down. He doesn't need to take water with him, and barely breaks a sweat. He breathes normally, because he is able to use the least amount of oxygen necessary to get the job done. And that, he said, is the key to all his accomplishments: ruthless efficiency.

In his work life, Levine appears to be constantly on the go, alternating between Mayo's Scottsdale campus and the Arizona State University (ASU) campuses in Tempe and downtown Phoenix. Plus he travels about once a month to Mayo's headquarters in Minnesota, where he lived for more than twenty years before moving south several years ago. In addition, he is often working on one or more health-related grants. (During a lunch with his staff while I was in town, he discussed starting a "seed library," where people would check seeds out of a public library and return them in the form of produce.)

But if Levine is asked to be on a committee and he doesn't feel he can contribute, he says no. The same goes for meetings. But that doesn't mean he's an asshole about it, he added. And it doesn't mean he is constantly at work. Efficiency can also mean recognizing the importance of taking a break, having a drink, talking with friends, thinking, or napping.

Science—and especially the science of movement—has always motivated Levine, who is an endocrinologist by training. When he was eleven he collected pond snails (Joanne and Maurice) from Regent's

Park in London so he could analyze their movements in a tank at home.

Formerly overweight and bullied at school over it, he became fit because of science. When he was at Mayo in Minnesota, he designed a pair of "magic underwear" that he used to track people's movements, including his own, day and night. The underwear showed that obese people sat two and a quarter hours more a day than thin people. Non-obese people moved around a lot more throughout the day, he found, in a form of movement he calls nonexercise activity thermogenesis, or NEAT. This led him to develop a treadmill desk that people can use while they work. The benefits are more than physical, Levine said. The data are clear that people can think more clearly if they keep moving.

Despite his crowded schedule, health-related work is not enough for Levine. He immediately knew what I meant by a Big Thing: "It has to be something you're passionate about, and that passion has to be utterly sincere."

For him, the compulsion to write a novel occurred when he was traveling in India and came across a fifteen-year-old prostitute who was writing in a notebook. Learning of her horrific life and her efforts to transcend it through writing, he was impressed by her dignity and personal power. She inspired him to write his first novel, *The Blue Notebook*, published in 2009, in which he speaks in the voice of a child prostitute named Batuk. His second novel, *Bingo's Run*, is about a fifteen-year-old drug runner in Kenya.

At this point, he thinks of himself as having two full-time jobs: medicine and writing.

"Doesn't your day job suffer?" I asked.

"No, quite the opposite," he replied. "I would say I've become three times more efficient in my day job." The reason is that the two jobs are complementary, Mayo is very supportive of his writing, and he has been able to establish routines to support both. When he is working at his Mayo job, he knows his subconscious wheels are turning in the service of his fiction.

*   *   *

While in Arizona, I started to become anxious about finishing this chapter, which was due the following week. Granted it was kind of a fake deadline, but my editor had set it, and I didn't want to let her down.

"I'm starting to stress about this," I told Levine. "I'll need to work all weekend."

"You'll love it."

"Do you think I can do it?"

"Of course you can. It'll come. Your body will make it happen. Like I was sure you could climb the mountain when I saw you sitting there vomiting, I am equally sure you can do this." (For the record, I did not actually vomit.)

The reason he was so confident, he said, was that the skill set required was similar to the one I had used for years as a journalist. The milieu was somewhat unfamiliar but the materials were the same: sentences and paragraphs. I was building on my skills rather than learning entirely new ones, which would have created an even greater strain on my brain.

I had learned quickly that I was not going to be able to do substantial work on this book when I had a big story to edit or write at work that day. But Levine assured me that it would become easier for me to juggle both jobs as my brain became accustomed to my new habits and found more efficient ways of accomplishing my higher workload. His second novel, he said, was much easier to write than the first.

"You're actually going to use the stress of your deadline—and let's be honest about this: nothing would really happen if you didn't meet it—to collate your energy to push you forward and your chapter will come out."

Just enough stress, but not too much—it can be hard to find that balance. A deadline—even a self-imposed one, provided you take it seriously—can help provide just the right amount of constraint and incentive, without throwing the body into a tailspin.

"Stress can be massively beneficial if it's correctly applied and correctly utilized," Levine said. We're all built for a short-term hit of stress, he said. It's when it goes on and on and on, producing cortisol that collects in our gut (resulting in the "bad fat" we are constantly warned about), that it becomes dangerous.

I had certainly had my share of gut-wrenching experiences working on my first chapter—to the point that I ran to my doctor for antianxiety medication (which I didn't end up taking because it made me so drowsy).

Levine provided a charming interpretation of my early stomach troubles: "You were falling in love with your book! It's the same symptoms!"

But his colleague, Elizabeth Capaldi Phillips, offered a more scientific explanation. She is a founder of the Obesity Solutions Initiative, which is jointly run by ASU and the Mayo Clinic. She handles the eating part of the equation, while Levine handles movement.

As she explained it, my stomach was probably protesting because the stress of embarking on my book had put me in a perpetual fight-or-flight mode. "Imagine all of a sudden you're scared," she said. "There's a guy coming at you with a knife. Your heart goes bing-bing-bing-bing-bing. You're ready to hit the guy or run." At that moment all your blood rushes to your brain, your heart, and your extremities. Digestion is a low priority.

Stress, Phillips explained, is like an "inside intruder" causing your body to suck blood away from the digestive area, and digestion needs relaxation and blood (see Belisa Vranich, above, on the subject of oxygen). There might as well be somebody inside your brain with a knife. No wonder the tummy and the bowels protest when the imaginary inside intruder invades.

Phillips is a cook and a foodie who studies the psychology of eating, and in 2016 she achieved her own Big Thing: planning and hosting a TV show about the psychology of eating that was produced by the public television station in Phoenix.

She proceeded to debunk some of the precepts that I had considered to be cornerstones of nutritional wisdom: Cooked vegetables are more nutritious than raw, she claimed; dinner is when you should have your carbohydrates (because they make you sleepy); emotional eating is actually quite rare. (But she confirmed two commonly held beliefs: to lose weight, it's all about portion control and changing your eating habits.)

To complete my Big Thing, I need a nutritional routine, Phillips said. The foods can vary, but I should have protein at breakfast (say, a few hard-boiled eggs, peanut butter on toast, or a can of salmon— "I'm a big open-the-can person," she said), more protein at lunch, and those carbs, if I want, at dinner.

I'd been getting into the bad habit of eating a cinnamon roll for breakfast. That has to stop, Phillips said, because the quick energy burst it provides is followed by a crash and sudden hunger. Remember, sugar is short term—not good for a Big Thing.

It can take two to four months for the body to adjust to a new food routine, she said, but "you have more control over yourself than you think."

I am trying to understand what has happened to my body since I started writing this book. It has changed. First I was very excited and nervous and even panicky. Then I began to develop a monthly routine—both physical and mental—and my body liked that. It started to work with me rather than against me. The stomach pains abated. I think it helped a great deal that I consciously began breathing horizontally from my abdomen and pushing out on the inhale, as Vranich advised. This was much more beneficial than any drug could have been.

Because my own body was my subject matter, I started to pay attention to it, whereas before I had been disconnected from it. All along it had been giving me information and I had mostly ignored it. My teachers helped me realize that. Habits were ingrained in my body that were harmful, and they helped me work to undo them. I am still in the process of undoing them.

Right now, as I take deep breaths and become aware of my scrunched shoulders and gently try to unscrunch them, as I unclench my jaw and the rest of my face, I can feel my neck lengthening, and that feeling radiates down through my back.

As I took my classes, and talked to Dr. Levine, Dr. Phillips, and Professor Hedge about the physiological elements of completing Big Things, it all came back to this: establish a routine.

This is why so many Big Things never get off the ground. The hardest part is to start. William James had it right: you have to endure a sharp period of suffering at the outset.

You need to endure some flailing and instability before you find your footing and hit upon the right combination of movements that form the ideal routine. The routine—both physical and mental— helps the body off-load work that had previously been conscious into a reflexive, unconscious habit. This frees up the body to handle big thoughts and big efforts.

THREE

In Bed with the Big Thing

Some days it's too hard to get up and start working on the Big Thing. The desk is too far away, and it just feels so good to lie down. And then I think: Is there any way I can get this work done in bed? I gamely try various positions, but they all end up feeling awkward.

At some point I end up fantasizing about hiring someone to connect my laptop to a pulley in the ceiling. I would be able to press a button and the laptop would descend until stopping about a foot from my face. Then, while still lying down, I could lift my arms to type with barely any strain. I could drift off for a while and then, just as I awaken, record a rich mixture of conscious and unconscious insights. The cat would probably want to jump on the laptop and stare at me, so the apparatus would need to be strong.

One day, as I brushed this fantasy aside yet again, I had a more realistic thought: I could ask my posture teacher, Lindsay Newitter, to come over and show me the best positioning for bed work.

Lindsay knew me well enough to realize that this wasn't some strange kind of come-on, but I still felt a little shy about asking her to come to my bedroom. And in fact she said that this was the first time anyone had requested a bedroom (as opposed to a home office) visit, although people frequently ask her about sleeping and reading in bed.

In general, she said, working in bed is considered a posture no-no because the surface is so yielding (a firmer bed is better if you're going to do it), although switching the locations where you work isn't a bad idea. However, "If people like working in a spot I usually don't like to tell them not to," she said. Then the question becomes: How can you do this with less strain?

I got my laptop and we tried out some various positions. First I lay down with my head against several pillows. My knees were bent and my laptop was propped against my thighs. But that placed too much downward pressure on my neck and quickly became unsustainable. Lindsay put a pillow under my upper back and then another under my lower back and still another, smaller pillow behind my head to give me more support. The pillow on top of my raised knees was an improvement but still uncomfortable. I could see that this position was not viable.

So then I sat up more and Lindsay arranged my pillows behind me in a kind of cradle so my back was fully supported. I put my legs straight out in front of me and two pillows on my legs to serve as a makeshift desk for the laptop. Lindsay instructed me to release my neck back so my head moved forward and up. This made it a little harder to look down as I typed, but I could see that this position could work. She helped me find a position similar to this for reading in bed—one of the great joys of my life.

"Think about the space between the back of your head and the screen," Lindsay said as I sat in my pillowy throne. "Don't overfixate your eyes—think of them softening, be careful not to tighten your jaw or your tongue, and think of your legs lengthening," she said, reiterating some of the general lessons I had learned in my classes with her.

This position was also quite comfortable for writing by hand in a notebook. For writing by hand I could also sit cross-legged with my notebook on two pillows. However, lying on my stomach and propped up on one elbow to write was dreadfully uncomfortable, no matter how strategically placed the pillows were.

A metal laptop desk I had bought online, designed especially for writing in bed, was a nonstarter, it turned out. Although it was adjustable, we never could get it to align correctly with both my eyes and my arms. Plus, a bump on the bottom edge of the desk to prevent the laptop from sliding off was too hard on my wrists.

Armed with the new information from Lindsay, I tried writing in bed more often. But once I tried to make it part of my routine, I immediately began yearning to write at my desk, effectively stopping myself in my tracks.

What I needed to make writing in bed workable was a maid, like the one Marcel Proust had. Her name was Céleste Albaret, and he could not have written the nearly 1.3 million words and seven volumes of *Remembrance of Things Past* without her devoted help.

Proust would not wake up until three or four in the afternoon. Then he would write until late at night, at which time he would often go out to socialize and gather material for his books. Then he would go back to bed, and the strict routine would begin all over again.

Partly Proust kept to his bed because of his severe asthma. But his bed was also the center of an elaborate ritual that released his creativity. Albaret wrote that he used his illness "as a further means of shutting himself up in his work and cutting himself off from the world outside. He wasn't afraid of illness. The only thing he feared was dying before he had finished his work. So he did all he could to erect as many walls as possible around himself.

"The miracle with M. Proust was his will power. And his will power was all directed toward his work."

The ritual was intimately bound up with coffee. Albaret had to buy a particular type of coffee from a shop in the seventeenth arrondissement in Paris. "The filter was packed tight with finely ground coffee, and to obtain a coffee as strong as M. Proust liked it, the water had to pass through very slowly, drop by drop." It was imperative that Albaret see to the coffee ritual and all the surrounding rituals in exactly the right manner.

In most of the rooms of his apartment, "the curtains were kept hermetically sealed and daylight never entered." His room was lined with cork to keep external noises out. He would tell Albaret he needed to rest, "but I knew very well that as he lay there motionless in bed, he was journeying forward in his book."

Many other writers, including Mark Twain, James Joyce, Truman Capote, and Vladimir Nabokov, have also worked from their beds. Writing for the *New York Review of Books*, the poet Charles Simic revealed that he is a member of this group, although he has no organized setup: "I lie in a chaos of tangled sheets and covers, pages of notes and abandoned drafts, books I need to consult and parts of my anatomy in various stages of undress, giving the appearance, I'm certain, of someone incredibly uncomfortable and foolish beyond belief, who, if he had any sense, would make himself get up and cross the room to the small writing table with nothing on it, except for a closed silver laptop, thin and elegant."

In the end, I decided it was best for me to make the supreme effort of getting up out of bed and walking to my desk to work on my book. Once in a while I do write in bed for variety, and it's nice to have the option, along with the superior pillow positioning I have learned from my posture teacher.

There's a part of me that needs to experience a demarcation between sleeping and working, I realized. I love to sleep, and I don't want to see my bed become a place where productivity is prized over rest. It seems to me I'd be better off simply using my bed to get a good night's sleep. Wouldn't this prime my mind to work more creatively at my desk?

Most definitely, said Matthew Walker, a psychology professor at the University of California, Berkeley, who has done extensive research on how sleep affects the brain and body.

His research has shown that sleep greatly enhances learning and memory. Overnight it will turn your brain into a kind of dry sponge that is primed to soak up information and encode new memories the next day. Sleep also in effect hits the save button on new memories and incorporates them into the neural architecture of the brain.

And there's more. Sleep can "cross-link and associate vast amounts of information together both old and new," Walker said. "By essentially marinating all of those memory ingredients together it can distill novel insights and creative solutions to problems you've been facing the day before."

It makes sense that no one ever tells you to "stay awake" on a problem. In fact, Walker has conducted lab tests that show that sleep enhances creativity by as much as threefold relative to an equivalent time spent awake.

History is filled with stories of people who found solutions to vexing problems shortly after awakening. Dmitri Mendeleev came up with the periodic table of the elements. Paul McCartney said the song "Let It Be" came to him in a dream. Mary Shelley got the idea for *Frankenstein* in a dream.

Creative inspiration or a solution to a problem may emerge from actual dream content, or the answer may come in a flash of insight, seemingly out of nowhere, but really it has arrived by special delivery from the backroom of sleep. It's yet another example of how creativity is as much about not doing as doing. More precisely, you have to accept that work is going on in your brain that you can't control. When you're not trying, you may end up making the biggest progress. But making yourself still enough and open enough to receive messages from that alternate workforce—so industrious, but so mysterious—can be difficult in this distracting world.

Nearly all the functions of the brain and body improve after sleep, and are impaired by a lack of sleep. During the night, the brain cycles back and forth through two main types of sleep: non–rapid eye movement sleep, which is deep and usually dreamless, and rapid eye movement, which is where most dreams occur. Things happen in the different stages of sleep to support different processes.

Sleep seems to be present in every species; it appears to have evolved along with life itself, Walker said. Because it requires shutting off one's waking consciousness and therefore one's alertness to impending predators, it clearly serves vital functions.

"Human beings are the only species that deliberately deprive themselves of sleep without any benefit," Walker said. But, I pointed out, their jobs may require them to skimp on sleep, so there is an economic benefit. True, he said, but when work deprives people of sleep, they pay for it in the form of lost efficiency, inability to focus, and reduced productivity.

He has also traced the emergence of a phenomenon he calls "sleep procrastination." This is where, when it's time to go to sleep, people deliberately create an environment where it is hard for them to fall asleep. More people are bringing their devices to bed with them, checking emails and Facebook posts, reading articles on their iPads or watching movies on Netflix. Not only do all these stimuli jangle the brain, but the light from the devices themselves prevents the release of melatonin, which regulates the sleep cycle.

Until I talked to Walker, I had never thought of my sleep as being susceptible to procrastination. I suddenly realized that just as I was prone to procrastinating in my work, I was doing the same with my sleep. Almost every night I read in bed, and I keep reading even if I start to feel tired. Usually I wake at two or three in the morning and have to turn the light off.

Worse, I have long been in the habit of drinking coffee before I go to bed. Although it doesn't seem to keep me up, it certainly causes me to wake up early in the morning for a few hours, before I then return to sleep.

I had never stopped to analyze why I was ingesting a stimulant at exactly the time when I was supposed to be winding down. After talking to Walker, I had an epiphany: it was all part of my pattern of avoiding the moment. Avoiding work and sleep through procrastination had been a misguided way for me to try to buy time—maybe even a way to fool myself into thinking I was extending my life. But to live a full life, and to get my Big Thing done, I need to catch the part of myself that is always leaping ahead of or behind the moment and bring it into the rhythm of what is happening right now.

Now I have (mostly) stopped drinking coffee after 3 p.m. At the end of the day, if I have worked hard, I feel a righteous fatigue. I still read in bed, in the marvelous cradling position that Lindsay taught me, but I try to be alert to the first signs of sleepiness, so I can turn out the light before I drift off. These small changes have made a big difference.

When you are sleep deprived, your ability to judge your level of impairment is also deprived, Walker said. So if you are working on a Big Thing, and you have other commitments as well, do not think you can give your sleep short shrift. On the contrary, you should guard and nurture your sleep.

Unless, I would add, you are a short sleeper, or the estimated one percent of the population that requires much less than the average seven or eight hours a night that most people do. Famous short sleepers in history have included Thomas Edison, Margaret Thatcher, Michelangelo, and Napoleon. There is a reason that Jim Levine, the very busy doctor at the Mayo Clinic, is able to write novels in his spare time. It appears that he, too, is a short sleeper.

From the time he was a boy, Levine was unable to sleep more than four or five hours a night, and he felt guilty about it. Because he didn't want to disturb anyone else in his family, he would sneak out of the house at around four in the morning and traipse around London. He saw a lot of prostitutes and drunks, homeless people and others who live in society's shadows.

When he was twelve he started joining a friend of his on her paper route. When she told him that a friend of hers "fancied him," he became smitten and began writing the girl love letters and poems, dropping them in her letter box at three in the morning.

The girl's parents became alarmed at letters showing up for their daughter overnight and called the police. Imagine little Jim's terror when one predawn morning he was accosted by three police officers who were lying in wait for him, expecting a fully grown pervert. He promised he would never do it again, and the police officers drove him home, unable to hide their amusement.

"One of the challenges for people who don't sleep very much is filling your time," Levine said. Many people would envy him his reduced sleeping requirements, but it sounds like a mixed blessing, I told him.

"It is a blessing, but you have to make it a blessing. Otherwise it's a terrible curse," he said. It's why he started writing novels. He could never have written his books without the extra waking hours that he has in his day, he said. Even after several hours of writing in the early hours of the morning, he can climb the mountain near his home and then juggle several projects at once in his day job.

When he does sleep, he is dead to the world. During the day, he can be overcome by a powerful fatigue—not the mere midday circadian dip that most of us feel—that will cause him to lie down on the floor and take an immediate nap. He has become an evangelist for naps for the rest of us, recognizing that we perform more effectively when we sleep and wake along with our bodies' natural rhythms, which cry out for an afternoon nap.

Whether it's day or night, Levine rarely remembers his dreams. "I'm living the dream!" he said, and I could tell he was only half-joking.

"The stuff you can do if you don't sleep very much is incredible," he said with his characteristic energy and exuberance. "Think about it, Phyllis—it gives you two lives!"

Contrast Levine's experience with that of Jean-Paul Garnier, a musician, composer, and writer who for much of his adult life has been unable to fall or stay asleep even though he knows his body desperately needs it. Garnier's chronic insomnia has shaped his creativity—and not always in a good way.

Born in 1981 into a middle-class California family, Garnier lost his mother to cancer when he was young, and he acquired a step-family after his father remarried. His father was a French literature professor before he entered the construction field, and instilled in his son a love of the arts.

When he was in eighth grade, Garnier ran away from home for three months, and he never did manage to return to school in any permanent way, so formally he has only a junior high education. When he was in his teens he started playing in a band, and that's when his chronic insomnia began. He's not completely sure of the cause, but part of the reason may have been the horrific nightmares he was having, which led to an aversion to falling asleep.

One of his worst periods of insomnia was between 2008 and 2010, when he was sleeping only an hour a night. Since he was awake anyway, he would work on his music. He was happy with how productive this made him, but he became so consumed with his work that he's sure it made his insomnia even worse.

When he wasn't on tour with a band, he lived in a place that had a basement music studio with no windows, and composed songs through the night. "I would work ferociously and was extremely prolific and it was great, but I would come upstairs and my roommate would be like, 'You've been down there for five days not eating or sleeping.' And I would just collapse."

He started feeling as if he wasn't a part of his own body. He also felt hypersensitive to light and other people's emotions. "You almost feel psychic when you've had that little sleep." Eventually he went to a psychiatrist, who thought he was suffering from anxiety and prescribed Xanax. Earlier in his life he had tried Ambien, but in both cases he did not want to rely on pills. Although it's wonderful to have a good night's sleep when you haven't had one for a long time, it doesn't feel like natural sleep, he said.

Now he's taught himself to fall asleep through a technique he calls color meditation. He'll close his eyes and follow the colors he sees through his eyes until he reaches a hypnagogic state between sleep and wakefulness. In that state an arc of beautiful visions appears to him, he said, and it becomes easy for him to fall asleep.

When I talked to him, he was working as an audio technician and facilities manager for a music studio in Los Angeles. Although he still had trouble staying asleep, he usually managed about seven hours of sleep a night.

He had taken a break from his music to work on fiction writing, including a science fiction novel. The color meditation, he said, "has been tied up in my writing process. I'll do these meditations to try to put myself in my characters' viewpoints." Then, after entering into a feeling of empathy with them, he generally falls asleep. He remembers that experience when he wakes up and can put it into writing. It's taken some experimentation to get the process down, but for his writing and for his sleep health it's been very beneficial.

Earlier, Garnier's problems with insomnia led him to experiment with a process called entrainment, which pipes one sound frequency into the right ear and another sound with a different number of cycles into the left. The idea is that you can induce various brain states—including sleep states—by varying the cycles that make up the difference between the two ears. (This process can also be done with light.)

Garnier set about creating a "Sleep Map," an eight-hour structure of shifting tones that would correspond to a perfect night's sleep. He even went so far as to buy a small EEG machine to measure his brain's electrical activity. He worked on the project for about a year, but in the end he abandoned it because the sounds, which are generally not found in nature, were somewhat irritating to listen to. Although entrainment might work for some people if they really believe in it, from a scientific point of view it turned out to be hit-or-miss, he said.

On the plus side, Garnier's insomnia enabled him to explore the more bizarre and unconventional sides of his craft, in part because he was up all night. With the Sleep Map, it also inspired him to put down his bass and start treating music as science. But when his insomnia was at its most extreme, it led him to feel doom-laden, and his work was fraught with negative emotions. "I think that lack of sleep and the confusion in life surrounding it led me to be nihilistic, and that was definitely expressed in the work I was doing," he said. "I'm happy to say that that's not really a part of my work anymore. Now I've found a way to learn how to go to sleep and get fodder for my work at the same time. And it's pretty guilt-free."

Garnier may have been wise to avoid taking pills for his insomnia. Matthew Walker is skeptical about taking drugs to induce sleep. "It's certainly true that when you take those medications you're not awake," he said, but it's a matter of debate as to whether you're in a natural form of sleep. And if you stop taking the drug, a rebound effect can ensue that makes your sleep even worse than before. There are now some very good nonmedicinal methods that promote sleep, including a form of cognitive behavioral therapy designed specifically for insomnia, he said. (Garnier appears to have come up with an effective method on his own.)

Sleep, Walker said, "is a remarkable feat of complex brain activity. And to think that a single pill could mimic that complexity is unfortunately just naive at this stage."

Causes of insomnia can be psychological or physiological, he said. Caffeine and alcohol can also be contributing factors. "It's important to realize that alcohol is a sedative and sedation is not sleep," he said. "By using alcohol you're actually just sedating your brain; you're not helping it sleep. And worse, alcohol will actually fragment your sleep throughout the night. It will make you wake up many more times." It will also block the generation of your REM sleep, and therefore your dreams.

I asked Walker: "What advice would you give to people who have insomnia and are working on a project?" You should really go to a sleep specialist to determine the cause, he said, but absent that, some basic practices of sleep hygiene can help. These include having a dark bedroom with thick curtains to block out the morning light, keeping your room cool, and avoiding both caffeine and alcohol at least six to eight hours before bed.

"Perhaps the most important thing for stable sleep, however, is a constant wake-up time," Walker said, including on the weekends. Having a different schedule results in a kind of mental jet lag that disrupts your biological rhythm all week long.

Walker is not among the sleep killjoys who say you should use your bed only for sleeping and sex. Reading in bed is fine, he said, but to avoid the melatonin-disrupting effects of devices, it's best to read from a normal print book in a dim light. And don't read something like a report from work that might make you anxious.

If you wake up in the middle of the night and can't get back to sleep after fifteen or twenty minutes, go into another room and read something relaxing like a magazine, he said. Otherwise, "your brain will start to associate being in bed with being awake, and you need to break that association."

It's a myth that depriving yourself of sleep can make you wildly creative, he said. Rather, it can lead to mental illness and even suicide. Sleep is essential to your mental health, he said—and, it seems clear, to your creative health. Better to keep dreams on the inside and try to remember them rather than force them outside in the form of sleep-deprived hallucinations.

Deirdre Barrett, a clinical psychologist who teaches at Harvard Medical School, is among those who believe that dreams offer a rich source of creative inspiration. In her book *The Committee of Sleep*, she provides compelling examples of artists, scientists, and athletes who have been able to use their dreams to achieve breakthroughs.

It's all very well to talk about harnessing our dreams, but remembering them can be difficult. When I try to record one of my dreams, I told Barrett in an interview, I either don't remember it at all or "I feel like I'm uprooting it from its natural soil. In my head it's there in all its complexity and bizarreness, and when I put it down on paper there's so much that is missing." So, I asked her, is there still value in recording your dreams on paper?

Yes, she said. For one thing, the mere act of writing a dream down will help you remember more of it. Chances are, if you wake up in the middle of the night and think, Wow, that's such a dramatic dream, there's no way I'll forget it, nevertheless by morning you will probably have forgotten it. And especially for writers, writing down dreams can be a fruitful challenge, she said. Visual artists in particular may choose to draw their dreams: "You really do find people saying 'I don't know how to describe this. I don't have words for this.'"

In *The Committee of Sleep* Barrett describes several dream "incubation rituals" that can be used both for personal problem solving and to make headway with creative projects:

- Write down the creative goal or problem in a brief phrase or sentence and place it near the bed.
- Go over the problem for two or three minutes, last thing before you turn out the lights. If possible, visualize it as a concrete image, or gather actual objects that are connected to the issue.
- Just as you are falling asleep, tell yourself you want to dream about the issue.
- Keep a pen and paper on the nightstand. Just as you are falling asleep, visualize yourself "dreaming about the problem, awakening and writing on the bedside note pad." (Some visual artists tell themselves they want to dream about an image that will be the subject of their next painting, she said. They may picture a blank canvas or literally place a blank canvas on an easel in front of the bed.)

- Upon awakening, lie quietly before getting out of bed. Note whether there is any trace of a recalled dream and invite more of the dream to return if possible. Write it down.

Barrett has conducted interviews with people in both the arts and sciences, asking them if they ever had a dream that helped them solve a problem in their work. Among the people who said yes, many said in retrospect they could see that the problem often required a solution that defied conventional wisdom. A nontraditional approach was just what a bizarre, hallucinatory dream could provide.

One of the most famous examples of this, she said, involves the nineteenth-century chemist August Kekulé, who knew that benzene molecules were made up of atoms but didn't know how they were arranged. It was before the invention of microscopes and he was trying to arrange the molecules in a straight line or an angle, which was all that scientists knew how to do. He fell asleep and dreamed of atoms dancing in front of him until they formed snakes, and then one of the snakes grabbed its tail. He woke up and realized that the structure of benzene was a closed ring.

The brain's secondary visual cortex is more active during dream sleep, Barrett said—not the part that processes from the eyes (which, of course, are closed during sleep), but the part that makes sense of all the imagery. With the primary visual cortex inactive, the secondary visual cortex runs wild with internal imaginings. Dreams are probably serving many different functions at the same time. Research has shown that REM sleep restores important chemicals in the brain, restoring neurotransmitters while our eyes are closed.

The prefrontal cortex right behind our forehead is much less active during REM sleep, Barrett said, and that is a big reason we're not as rational and linear in our dreams. This state also allows us not to question bizarre things.

Then there is lucid dreaming, which is loosely defined as any kind of dream in which you know you are dreaming. Lucid dreaming brings the prefrontal cortex more into the picture.

Some people try to train themselves to go from knowing they are having a dream (which is a form of lucid dreaming) to controlling the content of the dream, but it's easier to try to influence dreams in other ways, such as by consciously going over a problem before falling asleep, Barrett said.

Lucid dreaming scares me, I told her: "I almost don't want to mess with my mind that way. I kind of want to have it do its thing because it knows what it's doing." I'd rather keep more of a separation between my conscious and unconscious mind.

Barrett said that fears about conscious control of unconscious dreams are probably unwarranted because the dreaming mind will do what it wants to do most of the time. "The effects of waking requests to influence dreams are going to be pretty mild and change the brain state only briefly and transiently."

When it comes to interpreting a dream, identify the main dramatic element and the emotions you feel and ask yourself what they most remind you of in waking life, Barrett said. Sometimes, if you feel the interpretation is right, you might feel a kind of click in your body.

Dream interpretation is worth cultivating, and it improves with practice, she said. You can do it on your own, although enlisting a therapist or joining a dream group may help you overcome blocks that your psyche cannot penetrate on its own.

In the Torah, it is said that an uninterpreted dream is like an unread letter, but Barrett doesn't think all dreams hold deep meaning. Some dreams are just recycling and regurgitating trivial and repetitive information of the day before, she believes.

That was decidedly not the case with a dream she had when she was writing *The Committee of Sleep* and trying to decide on one of two alternate structures for a chapter. She had a dream where she was flying over clear ocean water and could see coral reef structures and tropical fish underneath. But she could also see blue sky and clouds being reflected on the surface of the water. She woke up and realized that her chapter needed to be a hybrid of the two versions she was considering, rather than one or the other.

To understand more about the mysterious world of dreams, I visited Anne Cutler, a psychoanalyst in New York's Greenwich Village who has studied dream interpretation and uses it with her patients. Psychoanalysis, of course, was originated by Sigmund Freud, whose pioneering book *The Interpretation of Dreams* laid the groundwork for dream therapy. Taking dream work even further was Carl Jung, who broke with Freud over his insistence on seeing a sexual meaning in most dreams. Jung saw dreams as offering pathways to personal growth, and he also posited the idea of the collective unconscious: structures that are shared by all humans and that flourish in dreams.

Psychoanalysis has gone through many iterations since Freud and Jung's day, but it still seeks to understand unconscious issues and conflicts "and it takes a lot of time and detective work to try to figure out what's going on under the surface," Cutler said.

I asked her: "Dreams are very bizarre and they're very personal, so how can you know what they mean?"

Dreams have a language of their own that's extremely visual and metaphorical, Cutler said. Also, "There's somewhat of a correlation between the level of disguise in the dream to the difficulty of the subject matter." A saving grace is that the most pressing themes tend to recur in dreams, so you may well have plenty of opportunity to try to unlock the secret.

Cutler believes that every element of a dream is meaningful (she differs from Barrett in this respect). "So it's really about picking it apart word by word, image by image, and trying to come up with as many associations to each element as you can, and then going micro into each image and then zooming back out and trying to see what story it's telling."

But when I write down my dream, I know I'm missing parts about it, I said. "Don't worry about what you're missing," she said. "Always focus on what you've got." (That's good advice generally!) Focus on creating a space where you lie there and try to recollect the dream, she said.

Sequence in dreams is important. Typically if you remember the whole dream, there's the introduction phase, which is the setting of the scene or the problem. Then there's information in the middle around a conflict, and there's some kind of resolution at the end. So you can look at it as a narrative in a way—although it's far from a traditional one.

Self-knowledge is powerful, and dreams have great reservoirs of it. They can help you understand what's working or not working in your life or your creative project—contrary to what your surface impressions may be.

Cutler's office was in a windowless basement and felt almost like a womb. It contained comfortable leather chairs and a Freudian-looking couch. I, of course, did not lie on the couch as this was a journalistic interview, but when I asked her to analyze one of my dreams to see if she could relate it to my life and my book, I felt the boundaries of our interaction starting to blur.

The dream I recounted to her was one I had had about four months earlier, while I was working on my chapter about age and creativity. I knew the moment I woke up that it was packed with meaning and made sure to write it down. As I retold it to Cutler she took notes on her laptop:

I had had a life-size replica of myself made, I think to get an idea of how others perceived me. I was keeping it in a cooler on ice. I remembered it was there and took it out and danced with it. The replica Phyllis was wearing a black dress that I had owned about twenty years ago. The replica and I stumbled a bit dancing but then we got in step a little more. I wrapped her up in my green bedspread like a mummy, but then I realized I'd better get her back in the cooler or she would decompose. Opening up the bedspread I saw that the chest already had red marks from decomposition and the facial features were blurred. I quickly placed the body back in the cooler.

I was in a big apartment and thought I was alone but actually people from work were moving in, including a woman from the *Times* I had recently met. Panicked, I went to check on my cooler, but it was gone. I worried that someone, like the *Times* woman, would think it was a real body and call the police. People were gathered around a body in the bedspread, but the legs sticking out were striped, and it was a man in there.

The main feeling was one of embarrassment that I would be caught owning a replica of myself. I was going to tell my friend Anne about the debacle, knowing we could laugh about it.

First Cutler asked me if I had any sense what the dream was about. I said no, except that it seemed to have something to do with my younger self.

Then she went through the images in my dream one by one quite rigorously, to get a sense of my associations with them. For example, the black dress.

"So the replica Phyllis was wearing a black dress that you owned about twenty years ago. What are your memories of that?"

"It was one of my favorite dresses. I wore it to death. I loved it."

"How did you feel in it?"

"I felt kind of sexy in the dress."

"And do you remember when you stopped wearing it?"

"Probably when I was in my late thirties."

The green bedspread was one I had bought a few years ago and kept in the closet most of the time because it was too heavy. And so on, until we got to the end, which featured my friend Anne, my best friend in New York.

I was nervous about how Cutler would interpret the dream: "It seems pretty narcissistic—dancing with myself," I told her.

"I don't think it was narcissistically driven," she said with a smile. "Let's talk for a moment about that time in your life when you were wearing the black dress in your thirties. Give me a quick picture of what your life was like then."

"I was in Minneapolis," I said. "I was working for a weekly business newspaper. It was a really fun job. We were very social. I felt popular there. I had a boyfriend then. So it was a good time in my life."

She looked over her notes and then put forward her interpretation. The dream, she said, has two main parts. By having a replica made, I want to develop some kind of objectivity about myself, not only to gain a better understanding of how other people see me, but to better understand myself. I deliberately choose to return to a time in my life that was happy, with the dance being an attempt to recapture feelings from that time.

Mummifying the body is a way to try to preserve that part of myself, but even in a dream that doesn't work, and the decomposition is a sign that I've lost that moment of connection with my past self. I can still keep it on ice to preserve it but I can't have it with me in the same way now.

The second part of the dream begins in the big apartment with the people from work. Police in a dream are often a stand-in for the superego, which contains all the shoulds and should-nots of the psyche, Cutler said. This part probably represents my fear that the two aspects of my life—personal and work—will collide. It will probably end with the police arresting me for trying to be sexy!

The first part of the dream is very intimate and growth oriented, but in the second part anxiety begins to develop as it becomes clear that I'm trying to pull something off that I perhaps shouldn't be attempting. I resolve my anxiety by planning to talk to my friend about it, which will give me some perspective on the situation so nothing will seem so grave.

(She had no idea what the man in the striped legs stood for, and I was glad she admitted it.)

I could see that the dream was about trying to recapture my lost youth, and that it also related to the book because I had been in the process of writing about age spans when I had it, and about drawing on the strengths of your younger years to complete your creative projects. It was a good sign that I had chosen a particularly healthy and happy time in my life to form part of my dream.

The second part of the dream reflected in part the fact that I was struggling with the book and that the success I was having with it was hard to hold on to.

I made an effort to write down my dreams as I worked on this chapter, using some of Barrett's techniques. Upon awakening, once I had lain still for a few minutes, I sat up in bed and wrote down what I remembered, even if it was only one image. Just as Barrett had predicted, the act of writing the dream down tended to conjure more and more images, until, more often than not, a complete narrative emerged in all its bizarreness.

Although I'm no expert, I did discern some images that were almost certainly metaphors for the book. Several times I dreamed that I had to leave on a trip and that there wasn't nearly enough room for all the books I had been planning to bring, so I left most of them behind. This to me was a message that I didn't need to read so many books for research. In one dream I entered a house where one room, I was pleasantly surprised to see, was completely finished, whereas before it had been under construction. In yet another dream, I had a big cleanup job to do, not only in the basement, but items were also piling up on the stairs. It was going to be hard to tell what to throw away and what to recycle, and there was a lot of work ahead, but I would do it.

*   *   *

After talking to all these experts, I understood more than ever that sleep needs its full due in your life, and that your Big Thing is more likely to thrive if you respect it. But among a certain swath of the population, it is considered a sign of weakness to give in to sleep.

"For many years I derived self-worth and satisfaction from actively cheating sleep to get the most out of life," Julie Flygare writes in her memoir, *Wide Awake and Dreaming.* When Flygare was attending boarding school in Massachusetts, she forced herself to get up after just four hours of sleep so she could play sports and be in the choir and still excel academically. It was in her family's DNA to push hard and get into the top schools. While majoring in art history at Brown University she kept a similarly punishing schedule and got top grades, but sometimes she found herself unable to stay awake in class.

Then, when she was attending law school at Boston College, not only was she falling asleep in class, but she developed another strange symptom: her legs would sometimes buckle underneath her when she laughed or felt annoyed. For a long time she thought the two symptoms were completely separate, nor did she connect the first two problems with a third one she developed: nighttime hallucinations that were frighteningly real, for example of a burglar in her room or a doorbell ringing over and over again.

Flygare is an avid runner, and when she went to a sports therapist for a knee injury she was finally able to connect the dots. In passing she mentioned the knee buckling. "I think I've heard of that," the therapist said. "It's called cataplexy." When she went home and looked up cataplexy, she saw that it was a symptom of narcolepsy, and that daytime sleepiness and hallucinations were also symptoms of the disorder. All of the things that she had been experiencing from different parts of her life came together under that term, she told me in an interview.

She went to a sleep lab and had electrodes attached to her head, and the doctor could not contain his excitement because her REM patterns were so strange. She was officially diagnosed with narcolepsy, which doctors believe is caused by a lack of cells in the hypothalamus that help distinguish between wakefulness and dreaming. As a result, aspects of dream sleep intrude into her waking life, and vice versa.

Normally when people are in REM sleep, the body paralyzes them so they don't get up and act out their dreams. In Flygare's case, her body gets confused and paralyzes her when she's awake. In a similar way, when she is sleeping, her brain processes her dream imagery in such a way that it seems like waking reality. Experts believe it's an autoimmune disorder that is partly genetic, and she has a genetic predisposition, she said.

Narcolepsy affects about one-half of one percent of the U.S. population. It is not curable but can be controlled through medication. Flygare's symptoms are much improved through a medication she now takes called Xyrem, which helps curb her daytime sleepiness, reduces her cataplexy, and helps regulate her sleep cycle. But she is still affected by the disease every day.

I thought how hard it would be to live that way, and I felt guilty in the middle of our interview when I realized I had cracked a few jokes and heard her laugh in a rather restrained way. She does have to watch her laughter, she said, although she can laugh more now that she is on medication. She also has to be more honest than the average person, because if she says something she doesn't mean it could result in a surge of internal emotion that causes her legs to buckle.

When she was in law school, all of her debilitating symptoms took a toll on her grades and her love life, and she fell into a depression. In her memoir she recalls lying on the floor of her father and stepmother's bedroom after a long bout of crying. "Narcolepsy is the worst thing that's ever happened to me, I hate it so much," she tells her father. Then she pulls herself together and says, "Eventually I'm going to make narcolepsy the best thing that's ever happened to me. I'm going to turn it on its head."

Instead of becoming a lawyer after graduation, Flygare decided to take a year off and write her memoir—even though her father was against the idea at first. She vividly recalls a moment when she considered pursuing a legal career and then closing her eyes and having a vision of herself lying in a hospital bed, her skin pale and her eyes made of marble. "It was as if I had no soul," she told me. She knew she would die inside, maybe even literally, if she couldn't pursue her creative passion.

"What do you call what that was?" I asked her. "Was that related to narcolepsy?"

"No, I was awake," she said. "It was a visual image of how I felt."

"Why was it so important for you to do this?" I asked.

Because, she said, she was tired of seeing narcolepsy being treated mainly as the butt of jokes in comedic routines. She wanted to try to get more people to understand narcolepsy through a human story. And more generally, she wanted people to understand the importance of sleep.

Though she acquired an agent, she was unable to convince any publishers that her story would resonate with a more general audience, so she self-published her book and was heartened by the response she received from other sufferers. Now thirty-one, she lives in Los Angeles, where she works full-time as a writer for City of Hope, a cancer research center. (They have accommodated her need to take a few short naps during the day.) She also founded a nonprofit called Project Sleep to raise awareness about sleep health and sleep disorders, especially among young people.

"So what should people's attitude be toward sleep if they are working on a big project?" I asked Flygare. It's important to make sleep a priority, she said. There's a perception that skimping on sleep is a form of willpower, but "you actually need your sleep to exercise your willpower."

"If you're doing things you're passionate about, I do think there's enough time in a limited day to get that done. You just have to prioritize very carefully."

So, I asked her, "Did you end up making narcolepsy the best thing that ever happened to you?"

"I cannot imagine my life any other way," she said. She would never have both published a memoir and run a marathon by the time she was thirty, she said. Before she knew she had narcolepsy, "I always spent time doing things to make other people happy." Now "I've done more with my life because I'm doing something I'm passionate about." And in the process, she's touched the lives of many others.

FOUR

The Intensity of Illness

On **September 17, 1925,** Frida Kahlo was riding a bus in Mexico City that collided with a trolley car. A steel handrail from the trolley ripped into her back and through her pelvis. Her right leg, already damaged by polio, suffered multiple fractures. Her right foot was crushed and her left shoulder was pulled out of joint. She was eighteen years old. From that point on, her life was shaped by her pain. Before the accident she had wanted to become a doctor. After the accident, she became an artist.

Even after many surgeries, Kahlo's injuries were so severe that she was forced to wear a steel corset. Her 1944 painting *The Broken Column* shows her in the desert, naked except for the steel rods of her corset. A Greek column replaces her spine, rending the two sides of her body. Nails are stuck to her face and body as tears flow from her eyes. Nevertheless, her expression is stoic.

In 2005, Dr. Fernando Antelo, a general practitioner in Los Angeles, was recovering from a car accident and came across *The Broken Column*. He felt an instant connection to the painting: it was as if another health professional were communicating with him, conveying in great detail the nature of her pain. He realized that the nails, for example, were different sizes and correlated to specific parts of her body.

The desert in *The Broken Column* is a symbol of how isolated Kahlo feels because of her pain, Antelo said, and her stoic expression could be an attempt to remain outwardly objective as she suffers internally.

Other paintings by Kahlo show internal organs such as the heart and can be extremely bloody. Some of her works reflect her anguish over her many miscarriages. Kahlo had an extensive medical library in her home, and her representations of internal organs are scientifically detailed. In a sense, researching and then portraying her pain was her way of gaining control over it, Antelo said: "It must have been very empowering for her."

In his own practice, Antelo finds that his patients often feel that no one understands their suffering. He tells them: I'm not going to lie to you and tell you I know what you're experiencing. But I'm going to try to bridge the gap between us and help you as best I can. "They appreciate the effort that you're trying to understand." In presentations he gives on Kahlo, he encourages his audience of medical students and doctors to listen to their patients in a similar way.

Pain is normally characterized by its unshareability. The novelist Carlos Fuentes called Kahlo "one of the greatest speakers for pain," because she was able to cross the barrier that separates the pain sufferer from all others: "Her scream is articulate because it achieves a visible and emotional form." Some see Kahlo's many self-portraits as a sign of her narcissism, but Fuentes sees it differently: "Through her art, Kahlo seems to come to terms with her own reality: the horrible, the painful, can lead us to the truth of self-knowledge."

Like visual art, music can also convey the pain of its creator. Some scholars have argued that Beethoven's tortured health brought tragic depth to his music. In his twenties, Beethoven began to go deaf. He also suffered from frequent fevers, painful abscesses, severe headaches, vomiting, and diarrhea.

Fearful over the effect that his deafness would have on his career, he tried to hide it from the world, while going to doctor after doctor seeking a cure. He was short-tempered and depressive anyway, and his deafness and other illnesses only made him more so. Yet he managed to channel his frustrations into his music. In fact, music was the only thing that kept him from taking his own life. "It seemed impossible to me to leave this world before I had produced all that I felt capable of producing and so I prolonged this wretched existence," he wrote when he was thirty-one.

Beethoven was never totally deaf, but he was basically incapable of hearing the sound of his own music. He used sound amplifiers and ear trumpets as best he could, but mainly he had to recreate his music inside his own head. He also "had a sense of virtual hearing through his fingers" through which his creative consciousness flowed, according to his biographer Jan Swafford. Although some of his alternative working methods led to miscalculations, they also appear to have resulted in fresh new musical structures. In fact, "much of his late music has an unbroken flow and long-sustained arcs," Swafford says, adding that some of it has an "inward, ethereal, uncanny aura" that projects "both loss and transcendence."

The idea that workarounds have their own value holds true for the author Laura Hillenbrand, who suffers from chronic fatigue syndrome and has been mostly unable to leave her house since 1987. Her bestselling books *Seabiscuit* and *Unbroken* were the result of detailed research that normally would have required extensive travel. But Hillenbrand found creative ways to work around her limitations. As Wil S. Hylton described in a profile of her in the *New York Times Magazine*, she persuaded an aviation buff to travel to her home and reconstruct a complex piece of World War II combat equipment, the Norden bombsight, in her dining room. These and other strategies enabled her to enter the world of Louis Zamperini, the bombardier whose life she chronicles in *Unbroken*.

"To function as an author, Hillenbrand has been forced to develop a unique creative process. Everything in her working life is organized around the illness: the way she reads, the way she thinks about language, even the way she describes familiar places."

Although it would be tempting to think that Hillenbrand has triumphed over her illness, in fact her physical limitations have contributed to the distinctiveness of her writing, Hylton says. "She has been forced by the illness to develop convoluted workarounds for some of the most basic research tasks, yet her workarounds, in all their strange complexity, deliver many of her greatest advantages." For example, because she can't visit libraries to read old newspapers for research, and because microfiche machines make her dizzy, she has taken to ordering vintage copies of newspapers from eBay. She reads them in her living room as if they were just delivered, and comes upon stories and ads that give her a taste of the historical era, lending her writing an immediacy that it might not otherwise have.

There is a great lesson in this. We all have imperfections and impairments—some more debilitating than others—that we need to work around. There may be ways to celebrate and even harness them, as many great creators have done.

Illness is a constraint, and constraints are required to get a Big Thing done. Deadlines are usually a good constraint. You might think of illness as a negative constraint. But in both cases, fewer choices are available, and therefore fewer distractions are possible. I remember an acquaintance telling me about breaking her ankle. She lived in a fourth-floor walk-up, and her life necessarily became circumscribed. This finally gave her the time to complete a cherished project: translating her Romanian grandmother's memoirs.

In her case, a bodily injury cut short her options and allowed her mind to focus on one thing. In other cases, the trajectory moves in the opposite direction: the body imposes a physical constraint because mental activity has become too intense. That may well have been the case with Charles Darwin, who took twenty years to write *On the Origin of Species*. His symptoms over that time included nausea, vomiting, intestinal troubles, headaches, weakness, dizziness, palpitations, and eczema.

Darwin's work was constantly interrupted by ill health. He took weeks-long water cures at a hydropathic establishment, which included enemas and douches, during which time he was mainly unable to work.

Theories abound as to what Darwin suffered from. Some experts speculate that he had an ulcer, or contracted a disease from bugs in South America. Others say it was arsenic poisoning, allergies, or lupus. Still others say his symptoms were mainly hypochondria, and/or related to anxiety.

It weighed on Darwin that his theory of natural selection was at odds with what most people believed at the time: that the earth's species had emerged from the hand of God. Instead, he argued, species had formed as a result of gradual changes within organisms evolving slowly over time. *On the Origin of Species* itself took many years to evolve, partly because Darwin realized that it would be controversial. In fact it was denounced as blasphemous when it was finally published in 1859, and it is understandable that he felt anxiety over its release.

At this point, it is impossible to definitively diagnose Darwin's condition. But it does seem that in many ways, illness served as a useful constraint for him. "The work was done in a tightly regimented way in between bouts of illness," said Janet Browne, a British historian of science who teaches at Harvard and is the author of several books on Darwin.

"Illness was a part of Darwin's daily routine," she told me. "I think he really felt ill. And then he felt so ill that he thought he needed to take a cure. And the cure forced him not to think. So actually it did cure him temporarily." His body was signaling, "This has to stop somehow," but he couldn't stop unless there was a reason to stop. To Darwin, nothing was so reprehensible as idleness—unless it was deemed necessary to improve his health, and so physical illness may have been a way to morally justify not working on his book.

Darwin was compulsive and self-absorbed, "and he examined himself very thoroughly, as if he were one of his own specimens," said Browne. That same compulsiveness drove him to make his book as complete and watertight as he could, which is another reason it took him so long to complete.

But for all that, Darwin was not very self-perceptive, she said. It seems that his body was communicating to him quite clearly, but often he did not know how to interpret the message. Keep in mind, too, that it was not so common back then to see the mind and the body as interlinked. But interlinked they are, in health and in sickness.

In the American Visionary Art Museum in Baltimore is an anonymous self-portrait formed from the trunk of a fallen apple tree. Called *Recovery*, it was made in the 1950s by a British mental patient who suffered from tuberculosis. The spare, elongated figure with a concave chest carries a naked expression of pain, anguish, and bewilderment.

The patient had shown no interest in art until he saw the tree on the hospital grounds and asked for help to drag it inside. Thanks to the art therapist Edward Adamson, who believed that art should be used to treat mental illness, the patient was allowed to use carving tools, which the hospital normally prohibited because they could be used as lethal instruments.

It took a month for the patient to whittle the wood into his own image. "The artist, in his thirties, committed suicide about two years after leaving the hospital," according to the museum. "This applewood figure is his only known work of art."

Pain, whether physical or mental, can be intense. The thought comes to the sufferer, even if dimly: Can I use this intensity somehow? I don't want to waste this pain. I don't want it to be for nothing.

At the age of fourteen, I began suffering from severe depression, accompanied by fatigue. At the same time I also began keeping a journal. I wrote in the journal two or three times a week for eighteen years. It is embarrassing and tedious and just plain sad to read some of the most self-pitying entries, along with the familiar expressions of adolescent angst. The first sentence of my first journal, written when I was fifteen, was "I think there must be something terribly wrong with me," which pretty much sets the tone!

But with later journals, I expanded my range. In many cases I simply attempted to record the events and conversations and perceptions of my life, and I am grateful to my past self now for creating this permanent record.

It didn't seem like a cohesive body of work at the time, but there it is now, thirty disparate notebooks—some hardcover, some softcover, some lined, some not—chronicling my life. When a beautiful and sensitive friend of mine died from alcoholism at age fifty-two, I read some of my detailed journal entries about her to her ex-husband (they had divorced because of her disease), and they brought back details of her life and personality that we had both forgotten.

After a few years, the journals began to pile up, and seeing the growing bulk of them gave me a feeling of accomplishment. Was this a narcissistic feeling? Maybe, but not only. The writing was a way to drain some of my pain, and to make sense of it. Here is an entry from 1977, when I was seventeen: "I have to have something to live for. I need more experience. I have the writing talent but I haven't got any vehicle for it. How can I write if I haven't lived? How can I live if I don't have a reason?" Clearly some part of me knew that the journals themselves were the vehicle and the reason. In fact, studies have shown that writing about your feelings can reduce depression and stress, prevent illness, and even help injuries heal more quickly.

The journals I kept were a way of climbing out of the utter hopelessness of depression. I started writing them in desperation, and in the process they became a habit. The habit enabled me to practice my writing skills, which became better as my depression also lifted. But when I finally received effective treatment for the depression in my early thirties, my journal writing pretty much ended, and I regret that, but I also see why it happened. When my mental health improved, I wanted to live more of an outer life rather than an inner one.

In her book *Touched with Fire*, Kay Redfield Jamison says that "creative work can act not only as a means of escape from pain, but also as a way of structuring chaotic emotions and thoughts, numbing pain through abstraction and the rigors of disciplined thought, and creating a distance from the source of despair.

"It is the interaction, tension and transition between changing mood states, as well as the sustenance and discipline drawn from periods of health, that is critically important; and it is these same tensions and transitions that ultimately give such power to the art that is born in this way."

Whether a mental illness is genetically based or environmental (and there is strong evidence that many mental illnesses are at least partly genetic), health professionals will often prescribe drugs. This can cause artists to fear that the creative well will run dry; the sufferer may become convinced that the illness is intertwined with the muse. This is why many manic depressives in particular stop taking their medication. But when the creative highs lead to despondent lows, too often suicide results, and the muse dies along with the artist.

As much as we seek a sense of joy and transformation in our lives, they don't come easily, and some turn to substances to find a quick path to those experiences. The connection between substance use and creativity is well known. Abuse, too.

Susan Raeburn is a psychologist in Oakland who, with Eric Maisel, wrote a book called *Creative Recovery*, about using creativity to emerge from addiction. One of her specialties is helping creative artists—especially musicians—find ways to finish their creative projects. She describes herself as "a huge music fanatic and a terrible amateur guitar player. In my sixties I'm still going to hear live bands, and most of my young friends don't even know who they are."

Raeburn was drawn to her line of work in part because of her upbringing, which was filled with both trauma and vitality. Her father, Lloyd Raeburn, was a big-band leader in the 1940s. He was also an active alcoholic, who died at fifty-two.

As a young adult, Raeburn never crossed over into becoming an addict herself, but she lost friends who did. Partly to make sense of her loss, she decided to become a psychologist, and in the 1980s she wrote her Ph.D. dissertation on the occupational stress experienced by rock musicians.

In her practice, Raeburn tries to show artists how their creative commitments have become derailed by their drug use. Often she sees artists after they've hit bottom and have come out of rehab, which is ideal because they've already done some of the irrigation work necessary to stay sober.

In the past, the conventional wisdom was that you could only treat patients if they were sober, but that thinking has changed, Raeburn said. Now she tries to reach her patients where they are, whether they are sober or using substances, or abusing them to the point of experiencing negative consequences.

At a certain point, use becomes abuse; biology kicks in and people become dependent, and that results in a loss of control. When someone is abusing a substance, the addiction will end up taking precedence over a creative project, she said.

She understands why people like to get high in the first place: because it's fun, it's relaxing, and it inspires them. A drug like marijuana can help people associate freely and come up with new ideas, but it's probably not going to help them by the time they need to execute them: "The buzz in one part of the project could really screw it up in another part."

Then there are the people who are so far into their addiction that all they do is talk about their projects and never work on them at all—their creative aspirations are just pipe dreams that feed into their grandiosity. "It's all fantasy at that point," Raeburn said. "People can certainly get stuck in there."

"Suffering is not creative," Raeburn said. "It's the transformation of suffering into art that's creative." People use substances as a shortcut to become transformed, and in the short run it's fun, but in the long run the addiction has its own agenda.

*   *   *

To get an inside view of addiction and the Big Thing, I thought of contacting Cat Marnell, a self-described "fallen beauty editor and renowned drug addict" in her early thirties who was writing a memoir called "How to Murder Your Life." Marnell formerly worked for the publications *Lucky* and *xoJane* but was unable to hold on to her jobs for long because of her drug addiction. A writing job at Vice also ended quickly. But when she was able to work, she turned out piercingly personal—some said overly confessional—columns on her drug use.

Marnell had been using and then abusing Adderall since being diagnosed with attention deficit hyperactivity disorder as a teenager. In a column about the death of Whitney Houston, she wrote: "Why can't we acknowledge that lots and lots of women abuse drugs? That they are a huge part of so many women's lives? Including mine?" This and many of her other columns were peppered with references to heroin, cocaine, OxyContin, Xanax, Adderall, angel dust, and alcohol.

I had images of meeting Marnell at a club at two in the morning and having to turn down offers of PCP and Molly. Instead, she wanted to meet at Le Pain Quotidien in TriBeCa in the early evening. "I'm flat broke and hoping you will buy me a salad," she said in an email.

"Of course I will buy you a salad!" I said. "And a beverage and dessert if you want."

"Amazing! I will be dressed in sweatpants and sweatshirt looking awful."

In fact, she looked as stylish as it is possible to look in a sweatshirt, with carefully applied makeup that was a far cry from the smeared eyeliner and lipstick and rattily glamorous attire, emphasizing her louche reputation, that I had seen in photos.

Although Marnell had received around two hundred thousand dollars as an advance for her book, that money was long gone, she said, spent on drugs and furniture. Her mother was now paying the rent on her TriBeCa loft, which she was also renting out on Airbnb for extra cash. "I literally only have this twenty dollars," she said, pulling the bill out of her pocket. That was all her boyfriend, an artist, was giving her as an allowance, she explained.

She had rented the nice apartment and bought beautiful furniture for it because she thought those things would help her write (she's not the only writer to fall victim to the furniture fallacy). "It didn't work, nothing worked, because I was taking so much Adderall. Every time I had writer's block, I was reaching for that pill. Every night I'd be so jangly, and all of a sudden I had a drinking problem." She'd drink at night and would then wake up with anxiety from not having written.

Then Marnell almost died of a heroin overdose (the friend who brought her to the hospital died a few months later, she said). Then she went to rehab in Thailand and while there started her book in earnest. When I talked to her she said she had written 70,000 words out of about 100,000.

The book was due the day she started it, when she began rehab. "I couldn't do it before then," she said. In rehab she got up at four in the morning and started to write.

What she learned in rehab was "to get up before your addiction." She knew that once she got home she wasn't going to stay sober, but if she just got up early to write she would be better with impulse control. She would be her best self of the day.

"Are you sober now?" I asked her.

"No, but I'm maintaining. So I like to believe. But it is working. I'm on Ritalin, which is like methadone as opposed to heroin."

Sometimes, Marnell said, she stays in bed all day and writes and drinks beer, letting the beer bottles collect on the bedroom floor. "This is how I dress all the time now," she said, waving at her sweatshirt. "I don't think about femininity" (well, that wasn't strictly true, I thought, looking at the perfect makeup). "I just don't care. I do have the ability to concentrate my energy but I can only handle so much."

A part of me felt guilty for wanting to meet her and kind of hoping to see a train wreck, which fortunately was not the case. But the fact is, she makes for a good interview because she is so unapologetic about her drug use. She definitely has an eye for the drama of her life. Her experiences make for great material for the type of "whack-job memoir" about addiction that she says she has always been fond of reading and is now writing.

When I talked to her, it appeared that she was well on her way toward finishing her book. But the long arc of a Big Thing is hard for an addict. "Addicts are reward-seeking," Marnell said. "When you talk about writing a book there aren't any immediate rewards, as opposed to a blog post."

Drug addicts are also lazy, she said. They certainly aren't the only ones, I said, referring to myself. After an initial burst of energy and resolve, I had fallen off the wagon and stopped writing regularly in the morning. Instead I tended to write in the evening, if at all, and could only keep at it with any persistence if a deadline for a chapter was looming.

I shouldn't wait until the night to write, she said. "At night you're tired—you work at the *Times!*" After work I do like to go home and have a glass of wine and maybe watch *Entertainment Tonight*, a *Seinfeld* rerun, and an episode of *Storage Wars* if it's on. And then I expect to work on my book? Well, sometimes I do, actually, if a deadline is near enough. But it would be so much better if I did it all in the morning and then had my evenings free to relax and enjoy my wine.

I'm reward-seeking, too. I'm not perfect, and neither is she. Our schedules aren't perfect, and what we write isn't perfect, and the final product doesn't turn out as planned. But it is worth the effort, for both of us.

She may well have a relapse, but the memoir is giving her a reason not to go back to that life. Writing about it helps her try to make sense of it. On the other hand, a life of addiction makes for great stories, and it's one of the reasons she got that big book advance in the first place. Will she try to create more unhealthy stories, supposedly for the sake of her art? It's a very fine line she has to walk, and she seems well aware of that.

*   *   *

Mental and physical illnesses are characterized by tension and a lack of ease. Most of life, really, is a lack of ease. If we did not feel uneasy, we could not move forward.

I think of the anxiety I felt when I first started writing this book, and still feel sometimes. And I think of the depression I felt for decades when I was young. I think of being too young to write a book and then wondering if maybe I was too old. It's a matter of physical and mental calibration. The calibration can never be perfect because then the result would be dull and predictable. Illness and impairment can provide a kind of negative energy, but only when they don't completely overwhelm the host.

Illness can be repetitious. We are told that it is good to live in the moment, but not with these things, this pain and continuous wanting. These repetitious necessities cloud all other aspirations for a time. How did we get to this place, where we could think of nothing else but this pain, or relieving it?

The people who transcend their impairments break free from useless repetition and enter into a new realm. The intensity of the pain itself causes them to do it, or the determination to accomplish their goal causes them to overcome it.

Nikola Tesla, for one, managed to work with, through, or around various bizarre and repetitious compulsions to invent such things as the induction motor and alternating current power. His obsessions included pigeons and the number three. He was afraid of dirt and germs and washed his hands constantly—in what would surely be diagnosed as obsessive-compulsive disorder today.

Some would argue that Tesla achieved what he did because of his compulsiveness and not in spite of it. It's an age-old question: Do the symptoms of mental illness themselves lead to creativity? Or does the creativity break free in spite of the illness?

Elizabeth McIngvale-Cegelski, a spokeswoman for the International OCD Foundation, has lived with obsessive-compulsive disorder since she was an adolescent. She has accomplished much in her life—including finishing her Ph.D. dissertation and starting a foundation. She is emphatic that her OCD symptoms were not helpful in completing her Big Things. In fact, they actively got in the way. Rather, she says, it was setting the goal of accomplishing a Big Thing that motivated her to obtain treatment and control her symptoms.

Growing up in Houston in the 1980s and 1990s, McIngvale-Cegelski was a bit of a celebrity, appearing in TV commercials with her father, who is known as Mattress Mack and owns his own furniture retail chain.

At age twelve, she began to have intrusive thoughts around cleanliness and disease, and began engaging in ritualistic behavior such as washing her hands hundreds of times a day until they were chapped and bleeding. She told her parents it was an allergic reaction to soap, but when they threw out all the soap her hands still bled.

She would call her mother numerous times a day to make sure she was safe. At school she was obsessively afraid that she would cheat, or be accused of cheating. She was afraid of being contaminated by books or other objects, not because she would suffer from a disease like AIDS, but because she would pass the disease on to others and it would be her fault.

Finally, unable to bear the suffering, she told her parents about her compulsions. They took her to professionals, who told her that her OCD was so severe that it was untreatable. It took more than two years for her parents to find a place that would treat her: the Menninger Clinic.

The clinic treated her using what is known as exposure-with-response prevention. She was exposed to her fears and anxieties—starting with the lowest-level ones—on a gradual basis, until she was able to experience them without engaging in ritualistic behavior.

McIngvale-Cegelski struggled with number issues. Her biggest fear, she said, was of not going to heaven, and she had a fear of the satanic 666, which led to a fear of the number 6 or any multiple of it.

Because her mother's age was 42, and 4 plus 2 equals 6, she felt that to protect her family from danger she had to engage in every activity of her daily life 42 times. That meant taking her first step back and forth 42 times, and the second one 42 times, and so on, and in the bathroom turning the faucet on and off 42 times, and then realizing that to continue to keep her family safe she had to engage in the entire set of these daily activities another 42 times.

In treatment she was exposed to the number 6 in various ways, until finally she would have to, say, write the number 6 on her hand and not think it meant she had the mark of the beast, and go out in public and buy things with the 6 on her hand without thinking that anything bad would happen.

"I still live with OCD every day," McIngvale-Cegelski said. Only because it was under control was she able to finish her dissertation in social work earlier that year (she is also an assistant professor of social work at Baylor University). Mainly she had to tame her fears of contamination, which, if they spiraled out of control, would prevent her from writing. To some degree she also had to mute her perfectionist tendencies. She still felt some compulsions to double-check and triple-check her citations, and was troubled by the old fears that she might be copying or cheating.

I asked her if ever felt she was harnessing her OCD to a positive end. Obviously, these are good qualities in moderation—you do want to get your citations right. I couldn't help thinking that it would be helpful if I felt compelled to work on my book in this way. But it doesn't work that way. A compulsion is a habit gone mad.

The problem with OCD, she said, is that nothing is in moderation. Some people say, "Oh, I wish I had a little bit of OCD," because then they'd be more organized or productive, but if you have true OCD it interferes with your life so utterly that you are unable to get anything done.

"I've never looked back and said, 'I'm glad I have OCD,'" she said. There is a condition known as obsessive-compulsive personality disorder, which is less severe, and may actually confer some advantages, but OCD does not do that, she said.

She knows that many creative people deal with mental illness, but on the other hand a significant portion of the population suffers from mental illness, so of course many creative people are going to live with OCD as well.

And here is where a Big Thing can help. To conquer OCD, you have to have a dream, McIngvale-Cegelski said—and for creative people that could be a big project. With a large goal like that to fight for, you have the motivation to overcome self-defeating behavior. If you don't have a reason to fight, it's too easy to get stuck.

People with OCD and other mental illnesses need to get proper treatment because "as long as your illness controls you it's going to be difficult to do anything," she said. She also believes, as groups like Alcoholics Anonymous do, that helping others is integral to healing. That is one reason she embarked on another of her Big Things: the Peace of Mind Foundation, which offers resources and advice to other OCD sufferers.

When you work on a difficult creative project, think about the people you are going to help, she said. "When you feel that there's some helping that's going to come out of this project that might be exhausting and debilitating to you, then there always seems to be healing there, too." I heard a similar sentiment from Julie Flygare. After Flygare suffered deeply from narcolepsy and came out the other side, she wrote her memoir, *Wide Awake and Dreaming*, and started a nonprofit to help others with the condition. A community of sufferers who had previously been isolated was able to connect because of her efforts.

That McIngvale-Cegelski was able to complete her Ph.D. while living with OCD is a major accomplishment. Finishing a dissertation is hard enough for mentally healthy people. According to the Council of Graduate Schools' Ph.D. Completion Project, only about half of Ph.D.

students in the humanities have finished their dissertations after ten years, with the percentages somewhat higher in the "hard" sciences and social sciences. The acronym ABD, for "all but dissertation," is affixed to people like a scarlet letter, as one student has put it.

The psychic overhang of an unfinished dissertation can have serious psychological consequences, with formerly healthy people experiencing depression, anxiety, and physical illness because of it. This was true for "Alison," a Ph.D. candidate (she did not want me to use her real name) I found through the PhinisheD website, where anxiety-ridden dissertation writers around the world can communicate, commiserate, cheer each other on, and sometimes procrastinate even more. She lives in England, where Ph.D. candidates are expected to finish their dissertation in three years (in the United States it's a little more flexible). She was able to get an extension on medical grounds because of her stress, anxiety, and depression. When I first talked to her she was five years in and getting closer to finishing her thesis on global education, but there had been some very dark days.

"It's given me such a negative view of myself that I didn't finish in three years," she said. "I look at people who did and I think, They must be better people than I am. I constantly think that I should have been working harder."

She said she struggles with perfectionist tendencies. "I never accept that what research I've done is enough," she said. "It can be really soul-destroying and paralyzing."

When she began working on her dissertation, her best friend died suddenly. A few years later she experienced depression, along with constant colds and stomach troubles, and she realized that she had never come to terms with the loss of her friend, so she went to bereavement therapy. After those sessions came to a natural end, she saw a therapist who diagnosed her with generalized anxiety disorder. With the help of cognitive behavioral therapy and mindfulness classes, she began to make progress with her dissertation. Her therapist helped her set smaller, more realistic deadlines and has helped redirect negative thoughts, such as imagining that her dissertation examiner would say, "Why didn't you read such-and-such book?"

When I talked to her she had finished 55,000 out of 80,000 words. She was heartened by the fact that "the more I read and the more I write, the more skilled I'm becoming." Still, she said, "I'm always overcoming this idea that it has to be perfect."

I caught up with Alison nearly a year and a half after I first spoke with her, and she did indeed finish her dissertation. One thing that "helped" her was an accident: breaking her foot. The injury kept her in bed and writing on her laptop. I asked her if it ended up serving as a useful constraint, and she said it did, although it was "a painful and expensive one, so I wouldn't recommend it!" Before she broke her foot she would feel anxious about where she should work—should she write on the PC in a spare room, on a netbook in the dining room, on a computer in the library? Confined to her bed for several months, she accepted that she had just one option.

"Diane," another Ph.D. student I reached through PhinisheD, took eight years to complete her dissertation, partly because when she was almost done, an academic panel told her she would have to rewrite it completely.

At her lowest point, Diane began having panic attacks several times a day. She tried drinking chamomile tea by the bucketful to calm down, but still the attacks continued. "I would notice that my left arm hurt. I'd think: Is this a panic attack or am I having a heart attack? And my heart would start racing and I'd be short of breath and I'd feel light-headed and dizzy, and I'd feel a cold sweat." She'd think: "I'm going to die right here in my chair and my thesis isn't going to be finished."

Feeling that she had no outside validation for her project, she would tell herself, "This is the stupidest project ever. It doesn't make any sense. I don't know what I'm talking about." She told herself she was lazy, and a loser. It got to the point that when she was walking around town she would think, "I should just jump off a bridge into the river."

"So much of my identity as a person wound up being embedded in the dissertation," she said. "If I quit or if I failed, it wasn't just a big project that I'd failed. It would be like my whole life was pointless." Finally, she went to her doctor, who diagnosed her with depression and prescribed an antidepressant. Once she started taking the medication, she was able to finish her dissertation in about a year.

The archaeology-related topic of her dissertation was personally meaningful to Diane, and she would do it again if she had it to do over, she said, but she would start taking the antidepressants much, much earlier.

It's common for Ph.D. students to experience anxiety and depression when they are trying to finish their dissertations, said Anthony F. Tasso, chairman and associate professor at the department of psychology and counseling at Fairleigh Dickinson University in Madison, New Jersey. The mental ills can tip over into physical ailments like stomach problems and back pain, and take a toll on the immune system, too.

For some Ph.D. students the dissertation takes on a life of its own until it becomes a monster. "They attribute a tremendous amount of power to it—more than it really has," Tasso said. It defines their identity to such an extent that it dominates their entire existence. As they fall more behind, they hope for a solution like a three-day miracle— where they have three days off and vow to work every waking hour to make up for lost time. This doesn't happen, of course, "and as day three approaches they come down with an illness—so it becomes a vicious cycle."

How sad that a Big Thing that is supposed to give your life meaning and structure can overwhelm your life to such a degree that it makes you ill. That appears to have been the case with Darwin, who may have unconsciously found a way to tame the dissonance that occurred as his body reacted against the demands of his mind.

But many Ph.D. candidates find themselves locked in a motivational paradox. Finishing their dissertation is so desperately important that they become certain that it will never be good enough, and therefore they do nothing. For some, not clearing that last hurdle relates to a fear of success or other unconscious beliefs, and this could stem from their upbringing, said Tasso, who includes psychoanalysis as part of his approach.

To pull his clients out of the dissertation abyss, Tasso reminds them that this is just one thing—yes, it's big, but it is part of a cumulative record of achievements. "Don't put too much pressure on yourself. Pace yourself," Tasso said. "You don't have to work on the dissertation from the minute you wake up till the minute you go to bed. Take a break, go have a relaxing dinner, watch TV. If you tell yourself, I've got to be working on this every minute I am awake, you're setting yourself up for failure."

Of course, not finishing a dissertation can have big professional and financial implications. But Tasso's advice can apply to other big projects besides dissertations if you have invested a large portion of your identity into them. If harmful mental or physical symptoms are taking over your life because of your Big Thing, step back and ask yourself: Am I letting this thing define my worth? Regardless of the result, you should continue only if the experience of working on it is worthwhile for its own sake and meaningful in its own right.

FIVE

It's About the Experience

In the past few years I have found myself climbing mountains, even though I do not consider myself a climber and have terrible balance. When I climbed the mountain in Arizona with Dr. Jim Levine of the Mayo Clinic, there were times when I was afraid and felt sick, and was unsure whether I could continue. But the immediacy of the experience—the no-choiceness of putting one foot in front of the other—was exciting, even exhilarating (especially when it was all over). That's one of the reasons Levine climbs that mountain almost every day. It's a powerful metaphor for his creative aspirations. It gives him a daily template for completion.

The feelings I have had while climbing—I don't think I can do this, I must go on, I can't let other people down—have played out in much slower motion as I have worked on this book.

When writing a book, some of the same questions arise as they do for mountain climbers: How fast and how far should I go? When should I rest? When should I admit that I need help? Should I quit before reaching my goal?

I had hoped to carry that metaphor down with me onto flat land, but in the middle of working on the first draft of my book, I started flagging. On a mountain, I must go on unless my body undeniably says, "No more." At my desk, it's so easy to stop.

After I finished a few chapters, I thought, This is too hard. I did not want to write this book anymore. Time is limited. I feel this more forcefully the older I get. Why was I spending it on this thing that I hated?

I didn't really hate it all the time, of course. Sometimes I did feel inspired and enjoyed it. But too often I faced it with dread. And then I procrastinated.

My body could sense my ambivalence and fear. Physical symptoms played out in much slower motion than they did on the mountain. But my body was always letting me know how things stood; that was the case with the Ph.D. candidates I interviewed, too.

The body is there to remind us that a Big Thing is not just a mental construct—it is also a physical experience in time. The posture lessons I took brought that home to me, but still, all too often I was seeing writing as merely a means to an end: a published book. I wanted to have written the book, not be writing it.

I realized that I needed more help to see it as an experience in its own right, like a trip or a pilgrimage or an expedition—even a vacation. So I talked to several people whose Big Thing was inseparable from one of these experiences.

Vacations aren't always Big Things. But they can rise to that level if they serve as a kind of marker in life, perhaps symbolizing our passage from one stage of life to the next—for example, the trips that young people take between high school and college, or between college and full-time work. A two-month trip I took to Europe alone after graduating from college was momentous for me, and was a chapter all its own in my life.

For Jeroson Williams, a trip he took in 2014 was a rite of passage of sorts, and definitely a Big Thing. Williams had just graduated from Morehouse College in Atlanta and was planning to go on to medical school. Before starting his studies, he traveled to South America with his friend and fellow student Taylor Harris, who timed the trip to coincide with the World Cup.

Williams went to an all-black high school and an all-black college in Atlanta. Where he comes from, people just don't travel to South America, he said. His friends were startled at his choice of destination, he said, and worried about his safety, but he was determined to have the experience. Harris was a more seasoned traveler, and he found himself inspired by Williams's wide-eyed energy.

Harris and Williams wanted their trip to be more than just a vacation where they relaxed and took in the World Cup. They wanted to make a creative project out of their experience, but they weren't sure what form it would take. "I don't feel normal if I'm not making something," Harris said.

They brought a video camera with them, thinking they would make some kind of a documentary that captured the pride of each country they visited. But when they had technical difficulties with the camera they switched to still photography, gathering ideas for how their project should be structured from the South Americans and other travelers they met along the way.

They landed in Lima, Peru, and went on to Chile, Argentina, Colombia, Ecuador, and Brazil. They resolved to go beyond the most-touristed areas and seek out the natives on their own turf. In Peru they visited the upscale Miraflores district in Lima and the other-worldly sand dunes of Huacachina. From the glitteringly wealthy district of Leblon in Rio de Janeiro it was just a short distance to the ramshackle favelas of Rocinha, where the streets became flooded with trash and buses got stuck in the mud after it rained. Scenes like these gave Williams and Harris a sense of South America's stark economic disparities.

Although they knew very little Spanish, they met up with a U.S. marine who did. A roommate of Harris who was also on the trip spoke some Portuguese, so they were able to bond with non-English-speaking South Americans.

Williams's friends, as it turned out, were right to be concerned. In the Brazilian favela, a young man pointed an Uzi at them and demanded their camera. Harris and Williams assumed that it was because this was an area where a drug cartel was active and it did not want any photographic evidence of its activities. Using the language barrier to their advantage, Harris and Williams refused to give up the camera, and they got a good photo out of it, too.

Despite the frightening incident, Harris and Williams returned to the favela a week later, when Brazil was playing Germany in the World Cup. They saw a group of children enthusiastically playing soccer while other people in the neighborhood were raptly watching the big game on televisions nearby. Harris felt that his photos of the scene showed how soccer gave Brazilians living in a harsh environment a sense of happiness and pride. Harris and Williams decided to call their project Orgulho, which is the Portuguese word for pride, and which contains within it the Portuguese word for goal—appropriate for the World Cup.

At a burger shop that had the best Wi-Fi in Rio, they ate about fifteen cheeseburgers over four days and compiled a video from footage they had taken on their iPhones to help them raise money for a Kickstarter campaign to create a high-quality photography book out of their digital images. They ended up raising $2,300 out of the $5,000 they asked for, and under Kickstarter rules, you don't get the money unless you reach the goal. But they were able to sell the book through a website they created, Orgulho.com.

The experience helped Williams learn to feel "comfortable with being uncomfortable," he said. "That's what allows you to grow." As two African Americans backpacking through South America, their perspective was unique, he said. With the exception of Brazil, it was rare to see any African Americans at all where they traveled.

From his trip, Harris learned that "things are not going to line up the way they're supposed to." He realized that he couldn't force his creativity, but rather had to let it come to him in the moment. The best photos he took were unplanned, as when he happened to walk to Copacabana Beach in Brazil; with Brazil out of the running in the World Cup, Argentines had taken over the beach. Just after Argentina won the semifinals, Harris found himself snapping his camera as he jumped up and down in the water along with three hundred jubilant Argentinian fans.

When I talked to them, Williams was about to start medical school, and Harris was creating websites and apps. Later, I learned, he began helping low-income businesses obtain loans through a non-profit called the Village Micro Fund. Whatever Williams and Harris end up doing in life, their trip to South America will continue to inform their experiences.

Whenever I talked to people about their Big Things, I always bumped up against a seeming contradiction: you have to try and yet not try. Within the context of a literal journey it became even clearer that these two concepts were not mutually exclusive. The journeyers I talked to had all committed to the overall structure of their experience, but they weren't sure what would happen once they were inside it, or after they returned from it. This was true for Dilshad D. Ali, for whom it was a Big Thing to go on the Muslim pilgrimage known as the hajj.

Ali was born in the United States and raised in the 1980s in Grand Forks, North Dakota, by devout Muslim parents who were born in India. Her father, a professor at the University of North Dakota, taught Ali and her two brothers Arabic so the family could read the Koran together, helping to keep their faith alive in an area where there were almost no other Muslims.

Ali married a fellow Muslim, and her faith stayed strong, although it was tested after she gave birth to her first child, who turned out to be profoundly autistic. "It was very humbling and stressful and difficult," she said. In 2005, when her son was four and her daughter was eighteen months, she was feeling particularly troubled—not to the point where she was experiencing a loss of faith, but where she felt a loss of trust in what Allah had planned for her and her family.

She realized that turning her back on Allah was not the answer—he had always been such an important part of her life.

They were living in New York City at the time, and her husband was a physician in training. It was then that she felt a strong calling to go on the hajj. God, she felt, was giving her an invitation. Women are not supposed to go on the hajj alone; it wasn't easy for her husband to get the time off, and money was scarce. But even though the need was not as acute for him, he supported her, and they made arrangements with a hajj group to travel to Saudi Arabia for a three-week trip in January 2005.

Her in-laws said they would take care of the children. But her father-in-law pulled Ali aside and said she should not go on the hajj with the idea that it would cure her son. Rather, she should go because she felt the calling, and to fulfill an obligation of Islam—all Muslims are expected to go once in their lifetime if they are able.

In the Muslim faith, Ali said, you are taught that there is a reason for everything, and when you pray for something, it is answered in one of three ways: immediately, and in the manner in which you asked for it; later, and in a way you didn't seek but that comes to make sense; or not at all, but for a reason that will make sense in the next life.

She realized that at first she had wanted to go in part because she had indeed hoped that Allah would "fix" her son. Once she understood that this hope was misguided, though, she was still determined to go.

The hajj has many rituals and rules. "We're talking about millions of people arriving for rituals done in a very specific manner. You can't just book your ticket and do what you want."

She vividly remembers the first time she saw the Kaaba, the House of Allah. It was the house toward which she and millions of other Muslims angled their prayer mats whenever they prayed. Now there it was, before her eyes. As part of the hajj ritual she circled the

Kaaba seven times, a symbol of spiritual devotion, and she felt the power and meaning of that.

I was seeing an important message in the hajj: limitations are required in order to move forward.

Ali agreed. There are many constraints in what you can wear and do at the hajj. The men in particular are limited in their clothing, with the requirement that they wear two simple, unsewn pieces of cloth.

These limitations open up a freedom inside you, Ali said. You are no longer worrying about your clothes or your status, but your spiritual state. You are not supposed to lose your temper or become frustrated with anyone around you, she added (a prescription that some do not always follow in such a confined space, but that is the goal, anyway).

She was struck by how humbling the experience was, and what a great equalizer. "Whatever you might have back in your home life, it's all torn down when you're there. It's three to four million people doing the same rituals in a very small space."

"Everyone who has gone for the hajj has a very personal and unique story about how it felt for them and what led them to it," said Ali (who as an editor for Patheos, a faith-related website, handles its hajj-related coverage). She felt strongly that going on the hajj would help her make sense of her situation with her son and find a way forward.

The hajj did change Ali, who now lives in Richmond, Virginia, and has a third child. She said she returned to America with peace in her heart. Her oldest son, now fourteen, is still profoundly autistic and nonverbal, but he is a wonderful and smart child, she said.

The hajj, Ali said, "brought a lot of trust back in what I could know and couldn't know and what I would never know." She now trusts that she and her husband are doing their best by their son, "and that God is there with us as we're trying to do these things."

*   *   *

For Ali, the hajj was first and foremost a spiritual journey. For other people, a journey is more overtly physical.

Physical challenges can be a form of self-discovery—and a test of your own limits. That is why some people find athletic races so challenging and fulfilling. And then there are those who live to go on expeditions, taking weeks or months to reach the highest peak or the farthest reach. One such expedition lover is Ann Bancroft, who in 1986 became the first woman to reach the North Pole on skis or by sled. She is a celebrity in Minnesota, where she still lives, and where I interviewed her.

As Bancroft described her influences and experiences, I noticed that she had a tendency to talk about past events in the present tense, as if they were still vividly there in her head. It became clear that she had learned some of her talent for vivid living from her parents.

Bancroft and her siblings grew up in a rattletrap old farmhouse surrounded by an orchard and alfalfa fields, in what was then considered "the country" and is now a suburb of St. Paul. The house was right above a waterfall, and that's where she learned to climb. "For us, going right out the door was an adventure," she recalled.

Her father worked as an insurance salesman in St. Paul, but being an outdoorsman at heart, he hated it. He needed to get out of town— way out of town—so he corralled his wife and four children into a family-size Big Thing: a volunteer stint in Kenya that lasted two and a half years. It was in the mid-1960s, and "it was unheard-of for a family, especially one with little kids, to just head off to the 'Dark Continent,'" Bancroft said. They lived on a piece of land outside Nairobi that was once part of the estate of the writer Karen Blixen (aka Isak Dinesen). Ann attended a local public school.

That trip was a marker for her—and for her family. "The world shifted for all of us," she said. When she returned to seventh grade in St. Paul she saw her surroundings through a different lens.

After she got back, Bancroft had trouble keeping up in school, and eventually it became clear that she suffered from dyslexia. This, too, informed Bancroft's view of the world. When she got the diagnosis, she no longer felt so much "like the dumb one." But the special tutoring she received, which required her to miss many regular classes, made her feel isolated. Except for sports, she hated high school, but she was determined to go to college so she could become a teacher.

Because of her learning disability, she continued to struggle in college and almost didn't graduate from the University of Oregon. But she's very directed. She knows where she's going, and she may not like getting there, but once she has a goal in mind, she's like the Little Engine That Could, she said.

She took an elementary school teaching job back in the Twin Cities in the 1980s and was a natural in the classroom. Because the pay was minimal, she also moonlighted at an outdoor-gear store in Minneapolis. That's where she met Will Steger, who was preparing for a dogsledding expedition to the North Pole. Right away she thought, I want to do that, and she drove up to Ely, Minnesota, to interview for a place on the team. She'd only been at the back of a dogsled once in her life, but the idea of going as far north as you can possibly go on earth was incredibly exciting.

All the other people training for the expedition were men, and culturally the time was right to recruit a woman to join them. That woman turned out to be Bancroft. Just as the team had hoped, including a woman helped bring media attention to the trip and attract sponsors.

The expedition required ten months of training, plus two months for the trip itself. Though she was only in her second year teaching at a school in the Twin Cities, Bancroft had the audacity to ask her principal for a leave of absence, and got it.

"So the training took longer than the actual experience," I said. Then I corrected myself. "The training *is* the experience, really." She nodded. Training in Ely "was the hardest thing I ever did," she said. "It was harder than the trip."

The training was rigorous and lonely. It was physically and emotionally exhausting. They were a ragtag team with little money and minimal equipment, and a group of dogs to train and care for. They had to work from dawn until midnight just to keep the camp running. They had to haul water from the lake and melt it, get the stove going in the big building, build sleds and sew harnesses, and feed and attend to the dogs, among many other chores.

At one point, some draft horses who had a fatal disease, but whose meat was untainted, were brought in to feed the dogs (they were preparing for the journey, too) and needed to be butchered. Bancroft was afraid she was being judged—would a woman be able to do this? So she plunged her hand into the carcass of a still-warm animal on a forty-below afternoon and learned how to butcher. She had no idea what she was doing.

Hearing about the extreme cold and the long hours and the intense loneliness, not to mention the amateur butchering of horses, I wondered if Bancroft had ever thought to herself, Why on earth am I doing this? I must be crazy. Yes, she did, she said—especially since there was no guarantee that she would end up on the team. Alternates were standing by to take her place if she got injured or didn't pass muster. "I never felt like my place on the team was secure."

But she was living a dream that she'd had since she was ten, and that made all the uncertainty and hard work worthwhile. She did make the grade, and after two more months of training and preparation on Baffin Island in Canada, they took a series of planes to the Arctic and set out on their journey to the North Pole, which took fifty-seven days. There were eight people and forty-nine dogs (one dog decided he didn't want to go and ran away when they were in Canada).

Six out of eight expedition members, including Bancroft, made it to the top of the world. Two suffered injuries and had to be flown out early.

Actually reaching the North Pole was anticlimactic, Bancroft said: "You're living like you lived the day before, only you're not traveling." But they began to celebrate as the plane with skis landed to take them to Canada and on to their homes.

Partly because of Bancroft's status as the first woman to reach the North Pole, the media coverage was intense, especially in Minnesota. But satellite phones were not in use back then, so during the trip Bancroft and the others did not realize just how fervent it had become. She was taken aback when she got off the plane in St. Paul on a warm May day and saw the governor and other state politicians swarming up to her, her face still swollen and stinging from frostbite.

Something like that will never happen to her again, Bancroft said. "Once you've done it, you're in a different place."

About a week after being home, Bancroft went back to her school, bringing a retired husky named Zap with her for show-and-tell. She discovered that just about every class had followed her journey, and that the teachers had all put their own creative spin on it. The geography class had charted her route. Students in the math class had calculated currents and distances. The art class had drawn polar landscapes. The music class had composed songs.

Bancroft loved teaching, but after the North Pole trip something in her was not fully synched. "I had always felt like my wheel wasn't spinning true," she said. That's when she had her epiphany: that she could be a teacher outside the formal walls of the classroom. "I could merge my two passions: teaching and expeditions." Shortly after that she left her job at the school to do just that. As the first woman to the North Pole, she had the platform to do it. She was the leader of a team of four women to the South Pole in 1993. Starting in 2000, she and the Norwegian explorer Liv Arnesen went across Antarctica on skis.

Bancroft has always differentiated between her personal trips and her public expeditions. This is an important distinction to make when you need to find sponsors, whether they are individuals or corporations. In the beginning, some people would say to her: "Are we funding your vacation?"

She understands that she is accountable to her sponsors and to the people who buy T-shirts and those who will be tracking her progress. In particular, she is keenly aware of serving as a teacher and role model to the hundreds of thousands of children who follow her journeys.

As Bancroft gets older (she was about to turn sixty when we met), she sees her expeditions more acutely in terms of legacy work. As long as she is alive, the trips remain in her own memory, and after she is gone she wants them to remain alive within other people. How will the actions she takes be translated inside the brain of a young person? Her actions need to be a reflection of her character as well as her achievements.

When I talked to Bancroft, she had just gotten back from India, where she was planning a big project with Arnesen, with whom she runs a company called Bancroft Arnesen Explore. They are organizing a set of expeditions to all of the continents, to include women from all over the world. In Asia, for example, the group will travel down the length of the Ganges through five Indian states, visiting schools, farms, companies, and citizens, with an educational focus on clean water.

Having an ancillary mission—like teaching schoolchildren about expeditions—is important, Bancroft said. During the lowest moments of her first Antarctic expedition, visualizing the 350,000 kids who were following her was like rocket boosters, she said. "It was different than wanting to do it for my family, wanting to do it for me, our sponsors even." She just couldn't disappoint that group.

The more I talked to Bancroft, the more I could see how going on an expedition was, in some ways at least, like writing a book. (She and Arnesen wrote a book together about their Antarctic experience, called *No Horizon Is So Far*, and that was actually harder than the journeys themselves, Bancroft said. Writing was uncharted territory for both of them, and they came to realize that they didn't remember the expedition in the same way. It was shocking to realize that they had experienced the same events so differently.)

Writing a book can take many months or even years of preparation, just as an expedition can. Both endeavors can require extensive research and the development of new habits and routines. In both cases, there are tedious and painful parts to be endured to make it to the final goal. And you want the end result to be meaningful and memorable—to yourself and others.

In both situations, too, there are deadlines to be met. But in the Antarctic, you have to be done by February, before winter returns with a vengeance. Mother Nature will not be giving you an extension on your deadline. She can kill you if you don't do the right thing.

I asked Bancroft: Does that kind of pressure attract you to expeditions?

Very much so, she said. "I like that immediacy. I learn about myself every time as a result. You're never the same person on any given trip. There is a continuum of growing and adding to the information trove that will benefit you if you acknowledge it going forward."

Expeditions demand tremendous honesty, she said. In everyday life, you may be able to fool people, but out in the wilderness, if you're not honest with yourself and others, nature will come back to bite you.

There's always something that goes wrong, something that doesn't go according to plan. During major expeditions, "you get to a crossroads somewhere along the line. Some people live to tell about it; some people don't. Your margin of error is small." She likes the singleness of purpose that emerges from that reality, and the accompanying lack of distractions. Here again the value of constraints—as they had with Ali and with the people who had found ways to work around their illnesses—became clear to me. Within constraints is room for a great deal of creativity, Bancroft said. "And surprises—aren't those interesting?"

Whether one is writing a book, or trying to make it to the top of the world, it's important to be gentle on yourself if nothing seems to happen on a particular day, Bancroft said. "Sometimes you're stuck in the tent because the weather won't let you move." Or you're stuck in your chair with nothing to say. It might be better to do nothing than invest energy in an effort that could leave you right back where you started, or worse.

With any big endeavor, you need to celebrate smaller milestones along the way, she said. But that can be hard on a polar expedition, "because you're traveling in a white world." At times the wind "has dusted away your tracks, and it's just the horizon line that goes all around you, so how do you mark progress?" The only way you can tell where you are is by putting the GPS in your armpit for an hour at the end of the day to get a reading.

I found Bancroft's description of the white world to be a powerful metaphor. You could view that world as a threat or an opportunity. You could look at the white world as the part in the project where you don't know what you're doing, or where you're going. Everyone I talked to who had worked on a Big Thing had reached that point at least once. It was a sign, I realized, that their project was worth doing.

Talking to Ann Bancroft in all her present-tense urgency led me to ask myself, How can I imbue the writing of this book with the purpose and immediacy of an expedition?

The posture lessons had helped a great deal, but more and more I could feel myself "endgaining," or straining ahead to the end result rather than living fully in the moments of writing. Vaguely I felt that the practice of mindfulness meditation might bring me back to the present. I had been avoiding mindfulness simply because it was all the rage—even business executives were doing it. But I was halfway through the first draft of my book, and it simply was not coming together as the cohesive and enjoyable experience I had been expecting. I couldn't help thinking that learning about mindfulness meditation could help.

A few days after my interview with Bancroft, and while I was still in my hometown of Minneapolis, I had breakfast with Dr. Henry Emmons, a psychiatrist who has been using the principles of mindfulness in his practice for twenty-five years. He has also written three psychology-related books, including *The Chemistry of Calm* and *The Chemistry of Joy*. So as an author, he had some idea of what I was going through.

Almost as soon as we sat down, I started spilling my woe to the doctor, who had a soothing voice, a calm demeanor, and thick gray hair that bespoke wisdom.

I explained to him that after talking to Bancroft, I wanted to try to make the writing of this book into more of a present-oriented expedition, and he approved of that idea. "But I'm really having trouble with that," I said. "Even though the book is halfway done, I'm still looking at the finishing of it as the purpose and the writing of it as just a tedious necessity."

"Would you like to change that?" he asked.

Of course I would, I said. He told me mindfulness could help me do that.

But, I said, I felt as if I would have to go to India and get a guru and become a Buddhist before I could reach that point.

"You don't have to do any of that," he said. It wouldn't hurt to get some training, he said, such as an eight-week mindfulness-based stress reduction class, because although mindfulness is simple conceptually, it can be hard to put into practice. But I could do it on my own, too.

Mindfulness, he said, is nothing more than "paying attention, being in the moment, and shutting off your judging mind."

Oh, is that all! Right away I could see there would be a problem, because I am a natural at judging. According to the Myers-Briggs personality test, I am an INFJ (introversion, intuition, feeling, judging). As an editor, it is my job to judge and analyze other people's writing. And in my own life and pursuits, I am great at judging myself—harshly.

Emmons described his own writing process—and like Bancroft, he spoke of the past in the present tense: "It's trying to bring myself into the moment, so I'm just there so I'm really expressing myself from a deeper inner place, not just thinking all the time."

To get into a writing rhythm, Emmons tries to clear a space for himself, both literally and figuratively. Then "I try to write from the heart as much as I can." He might even literally place his hands on his chest. He doesn't worry about being perfect. When he gets into his "heart space," he feels that his writing takes on a different tone— more reassuring and clear, as if he is talking to a friend.

This was similar to what I had learned in my posture lessons, where one of the goals was to open up the body so as to invite a richer mental experience. Emmons was familiar with the Alexander Technique and said it is actually a type of mindfulness practice. But it seems to me that mindfulness meditation is more about the head—or rather it's about using the head to get out of the head. A key component to achieving that paradox is to let go of perfection and judgment.

Mindfulness is the practice of placing your attention on something of your choosing, Emmons said. One of the simplest and most straightforward things to choose is your own breath, because it is naturally there, and it serves as a reminder that life is always up and down, contracting and expanding. You don't have to actively try to breathe from your abdomen (as I had done during my breathing lesson), he said. If you simply attend to your breathing, your breath will naturally deepen and slow down, and your mind will start to settle, he said.

I could picture doing this while simply meditating, I told him, but doing it while writing could be a real challenge, because you have to make an effort while you're writing. Isn't it necessary to strive, to try, to struggle, when you're writing a book?

You can put your energy into writing without striving, without forcing or grasping, he said. That reminded me of one of those typically paradoxical Buddhist phrases, the idea of "effortless effort." It also reminded me of what my posture teacher had told me about the way people tend to move in the world. Let the world come to you, she said, instead of straining out ahead of it with your eyes, your head, and your shoulders. You lose the moment if you rush out ahead of yourself.

"Just invite yourself to open up," Emmons said. "You can't force that. You have to invite it to happen. But if you can do that, if you can bring yourself back into that more open, centered space, you're working from a clearer mind."

"I'm an editor," I said to him. "So it's my job to be critical and judgmental. It's very hard to turn it off."

In this case, it's my job to turn that part of myself off, he said.

I've fallen into such a pattern of self-blame, I said. I love saying to myself, "I'm so lazy." It's part of my shtick.

"A mindfulness practice would be to really pay attention to that language, not to judge yourself for saying that, just to say, 'There's that word again. [The L-word.] I'm doing it to myself again.' Just by noticing that you're doing it, you want to try to let that go and speak to yourself differently, use different words."

"What would I say?" I asked.

"'I'm trying as hard as I can.'"

"But I'm not. I'm lazy."

"Do you really think that's true?"

"Yes."

"How do you define lazy?"

"I put it off." I pointed out that while on this trip to Minneapolis, I had planned to spend lots of time working on the book, but, although I'd interviewed several people, I'd done hardly any writing.

A mindful way to look at that, he said, would be to note that I did not do a lot of writing on my trip. "Lazy is adding a judgment to it which is not true."

"But maybe it is true."

"Do you really think so?" he said. "Because if you really think so, you're going to be stuck. You have to suspend your belief that that's true. From where I sit, a truly lazy person would not be trying to write a book when they're working full-time. A really lazy person wouldn't even work full-time.

"I think it might be true that you're procrastinating," he continued. "That's very different from being lazy. Lazy is you don't put out the effort. Procrastinating is you delay certain aspects of the work until a later point. Often it gets delayed until it becomes very uncomfortable, until it ratchets up the stress level." For some people, procrastination is necessary because they can only be productive when they're under a lot of stress, he said.

Procrastination produces a certain kind of feeling in the body, he said—a tension, a clenching, a vague sense of foreboding. The first step is to become aware that you are having that feeling. You don't have to try to understand it, just notice it.

"That makes sense," I said. "Most of the time you don't really stop and notice it."

"It's unconscious," he said. "And when a feeling like that is unconscious, it's going to win. It's going to have the upper hand."

I had never thought of procrastination in quite this way before—as a way to avoid being in the moment. And what is life except a series of moments?

On my path toward living more in the moment, Emmons advised me to get up in the morning and concentrate on my breath for five or ten minutes and then start writing.

"And then if I feel those judgments coming on try to push them away," I said.

"You don't push them away. You let them go. You have to keep observing them, knowing that they're simply thoughts. Be gentle with yourself. You don't want to give them too much energy because that just keeps them alive. You want to try to be really easy with yourself and know that this is something that everybody does."

"I can really start to change now," I said.

"You can start right now," Emmons said. A big experience for me, he suggested, would be to try writing this book without judgment.

And so I will try. Or rather, not try.

SIX

Giving Up, for Now or Forever

Typically books about creativity, even this one, talk about the value of persistence. Get your ass in that chair even if nothing happens. Just keep going despite the obstacles. Even if you fail it will have been worth it!

But the fact is, sometimes it's not worth it. Because maybe it's the wrong time in your life to do your Big Thing. Or maybe you shouldn't do it at all. Maybe if you do end up doing it, you'll look back on your deathbed and realize that it was a big waste of time.

I know that sounds harsh, but you need to understand your main motivation behind wanting to do a Big Thing. If your creative dream is fed mainly by unhealthy needs, then it probably isn't worth doing.

For many years I lived under the spell of what I call the Vague Big Thing. Mine was the conviction that I would write a great novel, with a complex and satisfying plot and finely delineated characters that would bring widespread adulation. Of course, for this novel to exist I would have had to sit down regularly and write actual sentences and paragraphs. I never did this, because not working on my book meant that it could remain great in my head. Why didn't they give out MacArthur genius grants for pure potential? I would have been a shoo-in!

In some ways this inactivity was connected with my depression. I had such a low opinion of my actual self that creating this shining potential-novelist self became a kind of temporary psychic refuge.

At least I was aware of this, although for a long time I was powerless to stop it. It helped that I came across the work of the psychoanalyst Karen Horney (1885–1952), who said that some people suffer from a neurotic need for things like admiration, approval, social recognition, fame, wealth, and power. If one of these needs comes to dominate your life, she said, it will shackle you with unrealistic demands—on yourself and others—and will prevent you from reaching your true potential.

I am convinced that Horney is not better known because of her unfortunate last name, which tends to produce snickers. Really, Freud should have been named Horney, not Horney. He was the one who thought sexual desire was the end-all, be-all of life—an idea that Horney resisted, as did Jung.

Horney posited that because of adverse influences, some people are unable to develop in line with their individual needs and possibilities. This leads to a sense of inferiority and a need to lift themselves above others. The neurotic person, incapable of taking real action toward genuine growth, creates an idealized image toward which most of his or her energy compulsively flows.

A neurosis can damage personal relationships, and because it involves the imagination, it has a direct bearing on creative work. "When we wish, fear, hope, believe, plan, it is our imagination showing us possibilities," Horney writes. "But imagination may be productive or unproductive; it can bring us closer to the truth of ourselves—as it often does in dreams—or carry us far away from it. It can make our actual experience richer or poorer. And these differences roughly distinguish neurotic or healthy imagination."

To function well, Horney says, "man needs both the vision of possibilities, the perspective of infinitude, and the realization of necessities, of limitations, of the concrete." A neurosis finagles its way around that challenge by combining a "longing for the infinite and the wish for an easy way out."

Much of life comes down to this: How do we handle our specificity in a boundless world? Being honest and realistic about our Big Thing is one way to do this.

True wisdom and maturity come with an ability to take our own measure—to acknowledge the constraints that come with our own individual type of humanness. For some, that acknowledgment may mean accepting that a Big Thing in your head will not turn out the way you planned, but it's good to go ahead anyway. For others, a realistic inner reckoning may lead you to conclude that it's best to put the brakes on this thing now, before it continues to oppress you.

It's true that if neuroses show up in small enough doses, they may actually serve as a goad, if an impure one, to get a Big Thing done. Narcissists with seemingly unbounded confidence may throw themselves with vigor into multiple projects, although the quality of the final product may be inferior because they overrate their capacity and are unable to work consistently, Horney says.

For more self-effacing types—like me—a neurosis can shut a creative project down by introducing perfectionism and procrastination. If you don't work on your Big Thing, you don't need to confront the fact that you aren't as good as you've made yourself out to be in your head. Deadlines can be an effective way to overcome this paralysis.

I guess I wouldn't be me if I hadn't carried around the idea of writing a novel for most of my life. But it clanked alongside me, oppressive and vague, serving as a kind of negative accompaniment to the things I was actually getting done in my life. Finally, when I was in my late forties, I participated in National Novel Writing Month, and along with thousands of other people around the world, I cranked out an average of 1,577 words a day in the month of November to come up with about 50,000 words and the first draft of a novel. That felt good, but I haven't gone back to the draft yet, and because so much of the true work of a book occurs in the revisions, I don't feel I can definitively state (yet) that I have written a novel. But I am much closer than I was before.

This book is much more of a commitment. I think about it and worry about it every day, but it doesn't oppress me in the same way that my Vague Big Thing did. For one thing, I know that this is exactly the right time in my life to be writing it. And even more important, my editor has given me monthly chapter deadlines to meet, so I am forced to sit down and take specific actions to complete it.

So often people allow their creative goal to remain a fantasy that arches out beyond what they actually do. Are they even capable of doing this creative thing that calls to them so beguilingly? This is where realistic self-appraisal is so important.

There are three main questions to ask yourself in relation to your creative goal:

- Do you have the talent/ability/skills to do this Big Thing, or the motivation to learn and practice them?
- Do you have the commitment and drive to work on the Big Thing at least somewhat steadily?
- Is it worth the sacrifice you will have to make, in time and money, to complete it? Maybe something else is more important.

As the renowned psychiatrist Adam Phillips says in his book *Missing Out*, the life that we lead is often accompanied by a parallel life that we live only in our minds, a wished-for life where we respond in the best possible way to all risks and opportunities. Phillips reflects that we can become so haunted by the shining possibilities of our unlived lives that they become more real to us than our actual lives: "Our lives become an elegy to needs unmet and desires sacrificed, to possibilities refused, to roads not taken."

A Vague Big Thing fits perfectly into this psychic setup. It is a way to channel one's creative longings into a fantasy life where a mythic double accomplishes works of genius. To handle one's longing by actually working on a specific thing is much more risky because prized illusions are likely to fall into the gap between imagining and doing.

The desire to work on a Big Thing can be very adolescent and narcissistic, said Howard Gardner, a Harvard psychology professor, author, and creativity expert who actually did win a MacArthur genius grant. There's a line that certain people with creative aspirations never cross, he said. It's only when you begin to understand that a major creative project is complex and difficult, will involve lots of effort and include elements that may not work out, and may fail in the end—only then does that mean you are serious. Having strong feelings and a desire to accomplish something are not enough, although social media is good at creating the illusion that this is possible.

Without sustained effort, a Big Thing is an empty vessel, built out of grandiosity. The more space you give it in your mind, the more it obscures what is really there in front of you: your real life.

Some people don't have a Big Thing at all—and in many ways, they're the lucky ones because they can be more gifted at living a real life.

Whenever I tell people—friends, coworkers, acquaintances, bartenders, other people at the bar, people I have just met at a party—that I am writing a book, and explain what it is about, I always ask: "Do you have a Big Thing?" And I quickly add, "Not that you have to have one."

A little more than half say that they do—usually it's a book, or an art or a music project, or a business or a charity. One woman, as an example, said she wanted to do a massive art project involving pillows.

But about half of the people consider the question briefly and say something along the lines of "No, I don't really have anything like that." They devote their creative energies to their jobs or their families, or both. They exercise, go out with friends, plan vacations, watch TV shows, read, and live day to day. They don't need to do a big extra project. I admire that.

After David Brooks, the *New York Times* columnist, asked readers to describe the things that brought purpose to their lives, an unexpected theme emerged in many of the responses. "I expected most contributors would follow the commencement-speech clichés of our high-achieving culture: dream big; set ambitious goals; try to change the world. In fact, a surprising number of people found their purpose by going the other way, by pursuing the small, happy life."

Readers spoke of finding purpose in being a good friend, being generous to others in small ways, of being a good spouse, parent, and pet owner, of lovingly tending a garden. These actions are small and incremental. They, too, add up over time. Whether consciously or not, these people see life itself as their Big Thing, with their daily actions creating a meaningful structure across time. This way of living spreads its own kind of influence, and in its humility and realism has more meaning than some grand dream that never gets off the ground.

One person I met who doesn't have a Big Thing is Andrea Loukin, who was a fellow student in the mindfulness classes I took to help me feel more present-oriented about writing this book. Loukin and I paired up for an exercise that involved one person talking for four minutes and the other person listening, and then switching sides. The listener was not to respond to the talker or ask any questions. As the teacher of the class, Paulette Graf, later explained to me, the exercise allows you to "just sit and listen and experience what it's like to just be present for that person." Too often when we converse, we're too busy rehearsing our own questions and responses to listen fully to what someone is saying.

Before the exercise began, Loukin asked the teacher nervously, "What if we don't have anything to say?" So I thought I would start, as I had plenty to say. I nattered on about my book—what it was about and the challenges of writing it—for almost the entire four minutes as Loukin looked at me with an immobile face, her eyes showing that she was deeply interested.

When it came time to switch sides, Loukin began haltingly, saying that she herself did not have a Big Thing, although she admired people who did. It was enough for her to work hard at her job and live day to day. Then she talked about how she might apply some of the mindfulness principles we had learned in the class to her daily life.

Just as she feared, she ran out of things to say, at about the three-minute mark. We sat there in silence until the four minutes were up—which I found refreshing but which she later said caused her some anxiety.

About a month after the mindfulness classes ended, I met with the fifty-nine-year-old Loukin at a cafe near where we both live in Brooklyn. I wanted to learn more about what it's like not to have a Big Thing in your life.

Briefly, like most adolescents, Loukin did have such a thing, when she was growing up in a middle-class family in Manhattan: she wanted to be a dancer. But since then, and really not even back in her dancing days, "I've never had a strong burning passion that makes me want to drop everything and do it." While majoring in English at Oberlin College, she took some dance classes but soon realized that if she pursued that life it would require too many sacrifices. "It seems really glamorous, but when you look at it from behind the scenes it's really tough. The commitment was more than I wanted."

After graduating she became an editor and a writer for a design publication, but she grew tired of the commute and the office politics. So in 1998 she started her own business: a public relations company for designers. But although starting her own company was a big decision, this wasn't a business with a capital *B*. This was a lifestyle choice. She was married and raising a son and daughter in Park Slope, Brooklyn, and wanted more flexibility to spend time with them by working from home.

Now that her children are grown, Loukin continues to run her business. She can afford to be picky about her clients, she said, and doesn't need to charge exorbitant rates because her husband, who is in the real estate business, makes a good living.

Her youthful dream of becoming a dancer was not a waste. Trim and fit, she still loves physical movement, although this has segued into yoga these days. She took the mindfulness classes because they seemed like a natural outgrowth of yoga and its exploration of the mind/body connection, and also because she has experienced some social anxiety and sleeping problems.

If you want to get psychological about it, you could say that some of Loukin's shyness and anxiety stems from her upbringing. She remembers early in her career having an opportunity to speak on public television, and her mother saying, "Don't do it—you'll make a fool of yourself." She ended up doing it anyway, loved it, and was asked back.

When I talked to her, she had just attended her son's graduation at Brown University, and she was struck by how much pressure there was on these young adults to find their Big Thing, and hopefully save the world, too—and this after the pressure of getting into and finishing college. Of course, she hoped that her son would find a job, but at the same time she just wanted him to be happy.

I admire Andrea Loukin's lowercase outlook, but I just can't live that way. And neither can Scott C. Reynolds, who has always had a burning desire to create. But for many years that longing was misdirected.

For years, Reynolds told me, he wanted to be on the cover of *Fast Company* magazine, celebrated for starting his own software company.

Like many tech types around the turn of the century, Reynolds became caught up in the mythology surrounding Steve Jobs and Bill Gates, and was among the subset of geeks who worshipped Shawn Fanning, cofounder of the music site Napster. "I wanted to be that guy, and be celebrated for creating something in the zeitgeist," he said when we met not far from his home in Brooklyn.

His fantasy was not unfounded. Reynolds was a successful software executive when he decided to chuck it all and pursue his dream.

That he had gotten that far was a testament to his skills and will-power. While very young and living in central Florida, he married and had a child. He soon found that working in a pizza place was not going to bring in enough money to support his family. With basically a high school education (he briefly went to community college), Reynolds taught himself computer skills. From being a tech support person, he learned to program computers and then became a software engineer and executive. When his marriage fell apart he moved from Florida to New York, continuing to work for the same company.

That's when he had a full-on crisis. He was spending all his time making products for other people when he should be making his own, he felt. First he thought he could create his product while still working full-time, but he just didn't have the energy for that.

So on New Year's Eve 2010, and much to his boss's dismay, he quit his job. Living on his savings, he vowed to create the next Big Thing in software.

He got off to a slow start.

"I took the first month and did nothing," he said. "I took the second month and did nothing. I watched every episode of *Everybody Loves Raymond,* which I had never liked, but it was on all the time."

Finally, in the third month, he started to meet people in the startup community and was eventually motivated enough to really hunker down and get started. He didn't want to waste his precious time off.

"So I sat down and I started . . ." Reynolds told me, and then he stared off into space. "Here's what's weird," he said. "I can't even tell you what the product was." At this point in his memory it was indistinguishable from all the products he had launched for others.

"What general area was it?" I asked him. "Do you remember?"

(Pause.) "No."

"I can't believe that."

"I can't, either. My life has diverged so far from that point. . . . I'm sure it'll come to me." But it didn't.

"If it was really something you were passionate about you would at least remember what it was," I pointed out.

"That's the thing I ultimately realized. It's like someone who wants to be a rock star to be a rock star—not because they love playing the guitar or they just have to write a song.

"I remember spending about a month with my head in the computer and being like, I hate this. I literally hate this. I don't want to do this at all." He still had an underlying drive to create something all his own and introduce it to the world, but this wasn't the right medium, he realized.

The funny thing is, what Reynolds really wanted to do was to write and do comedy, which are right up there with rock star and software entrepreneur in terms of being the focus of unrealistic dreams. In fact, it was the very topic of unrealistic dreams that sparked his interest in writing. While still working for the software firm he began writing a series of columns for McSweeney's, the literary website, called "Dream Jobs That You're Glad You Didn't Pursue."

The nineteen fictional columns, written in the second person, all begin with the title "So You Wanted to Be a . . ." and follow the career path of a person who aspires to become a spy, an astronaut, president of the United States, or a powerful executive, to name a few. The dream careers typically begin with glorious fantasies and end in deep disillusionment.

The rock star column is especially poignant, with the protagonist buying a Fender acoustic guitar in high school to impress the girls. He forms a band and gets some gigs and starts playing the local bar circuit while working at a Starbucks, all the while preparing to live the life of a star. He gets as far as making a single, but it only makes it to No. 77 on the charts, and it's downhill from there. He loses his house and his car and ends up playing his only remaining possession, his battered Fender, in the town square for stray dollars.

In high school, Reynolds and many of his friends nurtured the rock star dream, but then wisely came to their senses. A former boss of his is in a band, Reynolds said, and when he was younger he had dreams of putting out an album and going on tour. Now he's over forty with two kids and he and his friends are still in the band. "They play gigs and they have fun playing music together, and they approach the process very professionally but with no delusions."

Although the McSweeney's columns are fictional, they are all loosely—sometimes very loosely—based on career dreams that Reynolds and his friends had at one time or another. Three of them, computer programmer, comedian, and writer, are more directly autobiographical than the others.

Reynolds's final column in the series was "So You Wanted to Be a . . . Writer." This is the only hopeful one. The second-person guy really enjoys the process of writing. "One day, as if by magic, someone asked: What do you do? And you responded, naturally, as if it had always been so, 'I'm a writer.' . . . You were going to forge ahead, one eye on your bank account, the other on your word processor, and whatever happened in the end, you were going to make sure that you could look at yourself in the mirror and say you gave it all you had."

During his year off, Reynolds switched gears. In three weeks he wrote a film screenplay, a romantic comedy, and loved doing it. He started taking comedy classes and doing stand-up. Now, he says, he's on the path to becoming a film and TV writer.

At thirty-eight, he was working as a software contractor out of his home. It's his version of waiting tables—it gives him the financial freedom to do his creative work. He knows that the odds of selling a pilot or screenplay are very slim, but he's won a few awards and received some positive feedback from agents and producers.

I asked him, "Do you feel like you're being realistic?"

"I struggle with that every day," he said. In the end, though, he feels he is taking practical steps toward his creative goals. The comedy, although he enjoys it, is more of a means to an end, because many television writers start out as comedians and make connections from there. "I'd love to be Louis C.K., but that's not the path for me, I don't think."

When I talked to him he had written two feature-film scripts, two short-film scripts, and four sitcom pilots, among other things. He was currently working on a horror screenplay, "loosely set in my apartment." He works on it almost every day, and he enjoys doing it, even when it's hard, even though no one is paying him to do it. "No one can take writing away from me," he said.

Reynolds has this advice to others with creative aspirations: as long as you don't have grandiose delusions, why not work on a Big Thing? You just have to figure out what your threshold is.

"What are the signs of the threshold?" I asked.

With the software product, the threshold was when he asked himself, "Do I want to wake up tomorrow and do this again? And the answer was no. I don't care about this."

Reynolds's experience is a case study in extrinsic versus intrinsic motivation—a subject that Tim Kasser, a psychology professor at Knox College in Galesburg, Illinois, has researched extensively. When you are intrinsically motivated, you engage in a particular behavior for the fun, the enjoyment, the interest, and the challenge of it, he said. When you are extrinsically motivated, your goals are to achieve wealth, status, fame, and outside rewards.

A pure example of intrinsic motivation is a child playing. You wouldn't walk up to a three-year-old and say, "Why do you like to play?" Obviously, it's because it's fun.

The waters become muddier as we get older, but many creative adults work on a big project simply because they are drawn to it and challenged by it. Studies have shown that many animals, even rats, have an inherited need to explore new things that goes beyond their need for survival, Kasser said.

But it is all too easy—even if you don't suffer from a neurosis—to look beyond the creative activity itself and consider what rewards it might bring. Research shows that "people's extrinsic goals have been rising over the last forty years, and that's correlated with the extent of advertising that's in our culture," Kasser said. Social media is another force that stokes our desire for external rewards.

That's unfortunate because research has also shown that external rewards often undermine people's intrinsic motivation. The desire for money, fame, and status ends up clouding your enjoyment of creating, Kasser said.

But, I objected, even when you are intrinsically motivated, there's a certain point where a creative project becomes very difficult and it's just not fun anymore.

"That's about the challenge aspect of it," Kasser said. "I don't mean to make it sound like intrinsic motivation is always fun." When Edmund Hillary was climbing Mount Everest, there were many moments when it was no fun at all, he said, but the main goal of that expedition was intrinsic.

Citing the work of Mihaly Csikszentmihalyi, Kasser said that people experience what's known as a state of flow when there is an optimal balance between the challenges that a task offers and the skills that a person possesses to meet those challenges—and when the possibility of some future gain is not on the mental radar.

"Extrinsic motives are potent, don't get me wrong," Kasser said. They're what keep people coming to work every week. But research shows that when people become more focused on them, the quality of the product declines and they are less happy. If you start thinking, "Is this going to make me famous?" or "Is this going to sell?" it diverts your behavior away from what you personally and deeply want to express.

But deadlines are an extrinsic motivation, aren't they? And I have absolutely needed them to get my Big Thing done. Kasser said there's evidence that deadlines can undermine a creative effort. But if they are co-opted by the creator as a way to introduce structure into an intrinsically motivated project, rather than an outside force that controls it, they can have a positive effect.

It gets so confusing in your head—one minute you might be fantasizing about the fame and fortune your Big Thing will bring, and the next minute you might forget all that and throw yourself into your work. I asked Kasser: What advice would you give to people who want to ensure that they are pursuing a personal creative project for the right reasons?

"I think one thing they could ask themselves would be: 'Would I still do this thing if, when it came out, it was attributed to Anonymous? And I didn't get any money from it?' To me that's the fundamental question that it all boils down to."

That's a high bar! Would I finish this book if I knew my name wouldn't be on it and I had no hope of getting paid? The answer is no. On the other hand, I could never keep working on it if I didn't have some deep inherent interest in exploring this topic. I guess I'm just going to have to live with that dichotomy.

Kasser understands that the level of purity he is asking people to achieve is pretty much impossible. He wrote a book called *Lucy in the Mind of Lennon*—about the real story behind the song "Lucy in the Sky with Diamonds"—and he hoped it would sell briskly when it came out in 2013. It did not.

"I worked on that book for fifteen years," Kasser said. He started and stopped and there were many frustrating moments along the way. In terms of the outside attention it has received, "I may as well have thrown that book in the ocean," he said. "And you know what? I would have loved if it had done better, but I wrote the book I wanted to write. I answered the question that I set out to answer. And I learned a lot along the way."

And then he came up with what I think is the key to all this. It's very Buddhist and it goes back to the principles of mindfulness that I have tried, with varying success, to follow. If you really want your creative project to be meaningful, "you have to separate yourself from the outcome," Kasser said. It has to be first and foremost about the process and the experience.

Some of the people I talked to for this book felt that they had "failed" before they moved on to a project that "succeeded." But these concepts are transformed if you look at them in terms of a process. If you enjoy the process (at least some of the time) and are challenged by it and its inevitable frustrations, then it is a success regardless of how the outside world receives it.

These days many of us condescend to the word *hobby*. It's time to bring that word back into general use. To call your creative project a hobby, and to work on it humbly yet committedly, gives you more freedom to enjoy it for its own sake. Amateurs pursuing a hobby are more likely to approach their endeavor in the spirit of play. When a challenge arises, it is more of a puzzle to be solved, or a game to be played, than a threat to some conceit they have about their true identity.

Some people discount their day jobs in the belief that they are "really" filmmakers, musicians, novelists. Maybe that is so, or will be someday, but if there is a disconnect between what you say you are and what you are doing, you need to look within yourself more closely.

If your desire to be creative has remained vague for years, I recommend doing something, anything, in the way of a creative pursuit. At least narrow it down to a genre and from there to a topic. Trust in the power of incrementalism, and build in time for training and false starts.

If you continue to feel stymied, then it may be time to consider doing the unthinkable: putting your project on hold or giving it up for good.

Has your Big Thing failed to give you any intrinsic joy for years? Then ask yourself: Is it really worth it? Maybe the urge to create is misdirected and plays into a false self that seeks recognition at the expense of meaning. If a neurotic need is behind all this, you may benefit from therapy. Maybe you've lost sight of the fact that other things in your life are truly more important: your family, your job, your dog. Go burn some sage in a ceremony and give up on your big thing. And feel the weight lift off your shoulders.

SEVEN

Through the Ages

One day, when Autumn de Forest was five years old, she followed her father out to the garage at their home in Las Vegas, where he was refinishing some furniture. She asked if she could paint on a piece of plywood that was sitting there, and he gave her some brushes, a pair of gloves, and some water-based stain to work with. A short time later, Doug de Forest turned around and saw a painting that looked remarkably like a Mark Rothko. "Of course, I had no idea what a Rothko was back then," Autumn, now thirteen, told me in an interview.

Autumn wanted to keep painting, and her parents, realizing that this was likely to become a serious pursuit, bought her gallery-quality paints, tools, and canvases.

Autumn wanted to paint BIG; her imagination was more expansive than eight-and-a-half by eleven. "I didn't want to be confined in a smaller space," she said. "I wanted to be able to let my ideas run free." Soon she was working on paintings that were taller and much wider than she was. When I talked to her, she had already sold hundreds of paintings, many to seasoned collectors, for up to tens of thousands of dollars. She was also busy traveling the country giving speeches about art and motivation to collectors and school groups.

Autumn brings a youthful sense of play to her work, along with an artistic sensibility that is far beyond her years. You can see evidence of Picasso, Jasper Johns, Georgia O'Keeffe, Andy Warhol, and others in Autumn's paintings. But they aren't copies. "I take a classic painting and put my riff on it," she said. Her painting *Barbie Marilyn*, for example, owes an unabashed debt to Warhol, but in its resemblance to a Marilyn Monroe Barbie Doll goes off on a childlike tangent.

She paints with acrylic, or sometimes a material called encaustic, which involves adding melted beeswax to colored pigments (Jasper Johns did that). When she started painting, instead of using beeswax she melted crayons on a hot plate to achieve a similarly vibrant effect.

One of Autumn's greatest assets, her father told me, is that "she doesn't know what she cannot do."

In Autumn, both nature and nurture are at work in a big way. She is related to the prominent American painters Roy de Forest (1930–2007) and Lockwood de Forest (1850–1932). She has never had an art lesson. When I talked to her she was working on a series of Alaskan landscape paintings based on Lockwood de Forest's work, which was a refreshing change, she said, because she usually does pop art.

Doug de Forest is a composer, and Autumn's mother, Katherine Olsen, is an actress, but they have given over their lives to support Autumn's talent, managing her schedule and taking care of shipping, accounts, and inventory. Without their help, it would be impossible for Autumn to be so productive and creative. It makes you wonder how many other prodigies are out there whose parents don't have the means or the motivation to nurture their child's unusual gifts.

Certainly it has been profitable for Autumn and her family to devote themselves to her art. In addition to commanding impressive prices for her paintings, she has made licensing deals with companies like American Girl and Aéropostale. But in talking to Autumn and her father, I got the strong sense that although money was important, making the space for her to create her art was much more important.

Autumn is homeschooled, the better to accommodate her art and travel. I asked her if her parents had to badger her to work on her paintings. "No, no, no, no, no," she said with a laugh. She's excited to paint, she said, and does it whether she's at home or on the road. When she's not traveling, she likes to make time for three sessions a day of painting that can last from one to three hours each.

I was in awe of her passion and commitment. In my creaky voice I asked her: "Do you have any advice for me? I'm trying to write this book and I hate it! It's so hard to get up every day and work on it."

"Make a game out of it!" she said. Instead of focusing on the bad parts, the scary parts, focus on what's fun, she advised. Sometimes, she said, when she has two weeks to finish a painting, she pretends she has only one week instead: as a game, she tricks her brain into deceiving time.

When she works, Autumn says, she enters something called "the white room." "It's not a real place," she told me. "Whenever I am focused I go into this place and it's a room and it's all white, and there's not even a door. There's nothing in it. When I'm focused I can go to this place and I can spend hours there if I just stay in that one spot." From that spot her paintings emerge.

"Do you ever get frustrated?" I asked her. "Yes, all the time!" she answered in an upbeat tone. When she's not happy with the way a painting is turning out, she said, she tries to find a way of altering it rather than scrapping it. Sometimes "it turns into something that I never could have imagined and it's a million times better than what I had envisioned."

I could see why Autumn was in demand as a speaker. Her message: "Don't focus on how good you are. Focus on how much you love it."

I pointed out to Autumn that she must have an unusually long attention span for a child. To which she responded: "Quite honestly, I don't paint longer than some kids play video games." But again, her parents set the bar. "One of our philosophies around the house is to be a creative producer more than creative consumer," her father said. Autumn said she urges young people to "take this time, which is so precious, their childhood, to devote to something that they love."

As if that's not enough, she has also become involved in philanthropic causes, donating her paintings to charity auctions on behalf of victims of the earthquake in Haiti, the tsunami in Japan, and Hurricane Sandy.

On a video on her website, she describes herself at age five or six thinking that she had now passed through her "toddler phase," so she was at a point where she could try to help change the world. Unlike most six-year-olds, she was actually in a position to do that.

Autumn is an anomaly. She must have a very special prefrontal cortex. This is the part of the brain that enables us to plan and achieve long-term goals, and it doesn't fully develop until we are in our early to mid-twenties, said Earl Miller, a neuroscientist at the Massachusetts Institute of Technology. Individual brains vary, but in general children and adolescents have poorer impulse control than adults and tend to respond to immediate stimuli rather than delayed incentives. When you are young, you start out with more neural connections than you need, and your brain gradually pares them down to what's optimal.

The prefrontal cortex is the part of the brain most capable of abstractions and generalizations—putting many specific things into one category. "It can identify the common element in a series of things that may be different and identify them," Miller said. It also helps you come up with and organize the dozens and dozens of subgoals that are necessary to reach an overarching big goal.

The bandwidth of consciousness—how much information you can pack into your conscious mind—starts out relatively small when you're a young child. It reaches its largest capacity when you're a young adult. Then, when you get to be an older adult, after about age forty-five, your cognitive capacity begins to decline, until it reaches the same level that it was when you were a child, Miller said.

On the bright side, as an older adult you have much more knowledge; the ability to generalize about that knowledge leads to wisdom, which is the ultimate form of data compression, Miller said. So through knowledge and wisdom, older people can compensate for their declining cognitive bandwidth.

*　　*　　*

Autumn's story shows that it's never too early for a Big Thing to emerge. The American Visionary Art Museum in Baltimore makes it a point to show that it's never too late, either.

Most people think of old age as a time of diminished capacity, but late-onset creativity is common among visionary artists, said Rebecca Alban Hoffberger, who opened the museum in 1995. The museum states that one of its goals is to "confirm the great hunger for finding out just what each of us can do best, in our own voice, at any age." To that end, it nicknamed one of its exhibits "From Diapers to Depends."

Children love the Visionary Art Museum, and they gravitate to the mirrored Flatulence Post stationed between the men's and women's restrooms. Press a button and the (thankfully nonodorous) machine emits farts ranging from long, thin, and squeaky to short, deep, and resonant. The machine was designed by local artist Bob Benson when he was around eighty.

The art at the museum is quirky, playful, obsessive, surprising, poignant. The permanent collection includes a sculpture of the *Lusitania* made of 193,000 toothpicks, by Wayne Kusy, born 1961. The nearby plaque says that Kusy's first toothpick ship, made in the fifth grade, "taught him the great satisfaction that depends largely on immense patience and attention to detail." By the seventh grade, he had built three toothpick ships, "each more refined and realistic than the one before." But then, we learn, "these were destroyed in a freak accident when a door fell on them."

The museum's exhibits have included huge, fantastical whirligigs made by an elderly farmer named Vollis Simpson; self-portraits by Elizabeth Layton, who didn't start drawing until she was in her sixties; and work by Clementine Hunter, an illiterate African American farmhand who began painting in her fifties.

The wonderful thing about growing older is that you can reach a point where you say what needs to be said, without caring as much about what people think, Hoffberger said. And there is a richness of memory of life and experience to draw from: "When you really know what you're supposed to do in life, nothing was a detour.

"We often say that life experience is too big for words and it comes out in a nonverbal way as art from people who have never made art," Hoffberger said. She is drawn to people who feel compelled "to build the Garden of Eden in their backyard, and every morning they have a reason to get up and do that." They may not even consider it art, though others do.

Often the impetus for a late creative flowering is some great ecstasy, or a devastation. Layton began doing her unconventional self-portraits after the death of her son; she also suffered from depression and bipolar illness.

When I visited Hoffberger, the museum was exhibiting the work of Howard Finster, a Baptist minister from Georgia who started painting when he was sixty. He was repairing a bicycle when he saw a smudge of paint on his thumb that he realized was the face of God, telling him to paint sacred art. Finster told God that he couldn't paint because he didn't know how. God's voice inside the face on the thumb responded: "How do you know you can't?" Finster took up the challenge and made up for lost time by producing forty-seven thousand numbered and dated works of art until his death in 2001 at the age of eighty-four. He also built a huge outdoor sculpture space, known as Paradise Garden, that reflects his eccentric spiritual vision.

Like many visionary artists (they are also sometimes called outsider or folk or intuitive artists), Finster was self-taught. What his work lacks in technical expertise, it makes up for in exuberant variety and complexity. His art contains celebrities, historical figures, aliens, angels, and urgent sayings. Like Autumn de Forest, he was inspired by Marilyn Monroe, whom he proclaims in one work to be a "Woman Power from Earth into Space."

Hoffberger and I talked while sitting in a conference room inside a warehouse that holds artworks that are too big to fit in the main museum, such as a fourteen-foot-high sculpture of a pink poodle named Fifi.

The influences of childhood fascinate Hoffberger. For many children there is more sadness than happiness, she said, and a childhood trauma can be a powerful artistic force.

Hoffberger grew up in outer suburban Baltimore, raised by loving, supportive, and intuitive parents. She developed rheumatic fever when she was five or six. Though she was in physical agony, deep inside her bones, she came to feel that her illness was a blessing because it taught her how to transcend her body. She missed a lot of school and spent long days daydreaming and wandering in the woods. (Many inventors credit long walks in the woods as sources of inspiration, she said.)

She laments how "containerized" children have become these days. "They go from the crib to a chair to be strapped in to eat and to be strapped into the backseat of car and then to arrive at day care where the floors are all even."

Hoffberger was something of a child prodigy herself. She was accepted at age fifteen into Antioch College in Ohio without having to graduate from high school. But then Marcel Marceau, the mime, saw a film of her performance art and invited her to move to Paris to become his first American apprentice. She married three times, had two children, helped start a ballet company, consulted for nonprofits, and served as development director for the Department of Psychiatry at Baltimore's Sinai Hospital.

But the museum is her crowning accomplishment, so far anyway. Finding big creative works in unexpected people and corners excites her. "What I'm totally smitten with is fresh thought because it is so very rare."

Clearly, Hoffberger has been able to hold on to the wonder of her childhood. (In addition, she said, "I have no ability to edit how I think or feel at any time.")

*   *   *

The Harvard education professor Howard Gardner has demonstrated that a creator's childhood has a major influence on his or her creativity in adulthood. Using examples as diverse as Einstein, Picasso, and Martha Graham, he has shown that retaining a sense of childlike wonder can be a powerful force throughout one's life.

Einstein, for example, with his interest in explaining the universe "was, in a way, returning to the conceptual world of childhood: the search for basic understandings unhampered by conventional delineations of a question," he writes in his book *Creating Minds*. The Swiss psychologist Jean Piaget understood the importance of play and fantasy in the development of young children. As Gardner points out, some of the greatest creators seem never to have left this stage behind but rather tended it and kept it pure, while also integrating it into their more mature endeavors.

In her book *Creativity in Context*, the Harvard professor Teresa Amabile says that "families most likely to foster creativity in children are characterized by a low level of authoritarianism and restrictiveness, an encouragement of independence, and a somewhat cool interpersonal distance between parents and children."

Hmm. That reminds me of my own upbringing.

I come from Scandinavian stock (Finnish, Swedish, Norwegian), and true to that region's stereotype of standoffishness, I don't recall receiving many hugs or "I love you's" when I was growing up, but I did know that my parents had my back. They encouraged my reading and my early efforts at writing, but academically they never forced me in a particular direction.

When I started having trouble in school in fifth grade (I considered my teachers overly authoritarian), they took me out of public school and enrolled me in an all-ages "free school" near the University of Minnesota campus. They paid tuition for my sister and me to attend (around two hundred dollars a month—not easy to manage on my father's salary as a social worker), so the school wasn't free in a monetary sense. It was free in that the students weren't required to do or learn anything.

It was 1972, and the free school—called Second Foundation, after a utopian science fiction novel by Isaac Asimov—was in keeping with the spirit of the age: radical, experimental, nonconformist. Protests against the Vietnam War were raging a few blocks from us on campus. Hippie culture was in full bloom. The teachers, liberals all, took us to antiwar protests, and I wore a big peace sign necklace around my neck.

The four idealistic teachers at Second Foundation had a wide-ranging background in the arts and sciences. They encouraged us to learn new things and to teach classes of our own, but if we didn't choose to do those things, that was fine. I took lessons in science and literature, read Dickens and Dostoyevsky, and even tried to learn classical Greek. I remember carrying around Sartre's *Being and Nothingness*, which I didn't understand at all, and holding a class on the topic of nothing, which only one person chose to attend.

Back then I felt that my intellect had no limits, and everything I learned was fresh and deep and exciting. After a few years, I returned to public school and then came a period of adolescent darkness and confusion, and severe depression that continued into my young adult years. Once I overcame that, I focused on my journalistic career, and though I always aspired to write a book, I was also naturally indolent.

I didn't start my Big Thing when I was at that school, but the seed for it began to grow then. That year had an outsize influence and set the stage for what I am doing now. If we are lucky, we all have times in our lives when our stage of development and our personalities converge with the right external environment and historical era to result in a creative flourishing that deeply informs our later life—even if we aren't creative geniuses.

My Big Thing went by the wayside in my twenties, thirties, and forties. My guilt and disappointment over not doing it were high because that's when people are thought to be at the peak of their mental and physical abilities. But that, of course, is also when so much of "real" life happens, in the way of adult responsibilities and preoccupations. Remember, though, that the window doesn't necessarily close when you're past your so-called prime.

Just look at Linval Thomas. From the time he was in his early twenties, Thomas wanted to record a reggae album, but life kept getting in the way. When I talked to him by phone, he was in Kingston, Jamaica, preparing for the release party for his first full-length album. He was sixty-five years old.

During our phone conversation, Thomas frequently burst into song. "When I came out of my mother's womb, what was perceived to be crying was singing," he said. "That was my first composition." Growing up in Jamaica, he became hooked on reggae music; this was further reinforced by the early morning conga drumming he could hear coming from the Rastafarian community living in the Wareika Hill area nearby. Early on, Thomas wanted to produce the reggae music that he was hearing in his head, but the path to that goal took a detour when his father and stepmother moved to the United States. As he was preparing to join them, he found out that his girlfriend was pregnant. Eventually they married, and he moved his family to the United States, where his wife soon had another daughter.

It was his father's dream for Thomas to join the air force, and that is what he eventually did, rising to the rank of senior master sergeant. Music was always on his mind, though. He even went back to Jamaica while in his thirties and recorded some songs, but they were never released.

A second marriage, two sons, and a second divorce further delayed his dream. His first wife had primary custody of his daughters, but he gained custody of his sons. He had to give over his life to working and raising his boys. But as a devout Christian, he had faith—literally—that he would eventually achieve his Big Thing.

Thomas retired from the air force in 1993, while living in Illinois, and got a job as a teacher's aide for an elementary school. He became involved with the reggae community there and performed some local gigs. Some of the songs he had recorded received radio airplay. But he still hadn't accomplished his lifelong dream: recording an entire album.

Reggae was a staple in his household. "I said to my boys, I always told you that my passion is music. That's all I've ever wanted to do. And they said, 'We're sick and tired of hearing that, Dad. We don't want to hear that anymore.'" By which they meant: it's time to do something about it.

Finally, in 2013, Thomas put everything he owned in storage and found a place to live in Jamaica. Using his retirement savings, he hired musicians, singers, and technicians and recorded an album of his songs at Bob Marley's studio, Tuff Gong. (His voice has a rasp in it that wouldn't have been there when he was in his twenties.) He joined ASCAP and created his own record label to release the album, *Call Me*. After the album release party, he was planning to go on tour.

Of course Thomas wouldn't mind becoming famous and wealthy because of his album. But his main goal from the start, he said, was to create his own version of the reggae music he has loved since he was a child.

I wouldn't call Linval Thomas a late bloomer so much as a long, slow bloomer. That's the case for Sherri Kirkpatrick, too. When Kirkpatrick retired in her midsixties, she achieved her dream of starting a nonprofit organization to improve health in the developing world. Her organization, called HealthEd Connect, which she founded along with her husband, would never have been possible without a series of small, incremental steps she took across time. The stages of her younger life were in effect a dress rehearsal for the work she is doing now, she told me.

"I kept my dreams alive in small projects while working full-time but more fully unleashed my vision and energy when I established HealthEd Connect," said Kirkpatrick, who was seventy-one when I talked to her.

She was raised in Independence, Missouri, where she now lives and where her organization is based. It was the second marriage for both her parents. Her mother's first husband had died of tetanus, and her father's first wife had died of tuberculosis. Her parents' losses were a factor in shaping her aspirations: "As long as I can ever remember I wanted to be a nurse," she said.

She attended a nurses training program in Missouri and then moved to Stanford, California, with her husband, Jac, who worked as an engineer for NASA. They began fostering children from Mexico who had been brought to Stanford University by a charity to have complex surgeries. Visiting one girl's family in Tijuana after she had returned home, Kirkpatrick realized she had made a mistake putting her in her own bedroom all by herself. "She must have been horribly lonely," Kirkpatrick said, because the whole family slept in the same room.

Her experience with fostering sparked her interest in other cultures, and after the couple and their two sons moved back to Missouri, Kirkpatrick got a master's degree and then pursued a doctorate on the topic of health beliefs. Even before she received her doctorate she was named dean of nursing at Graceland University.

During the monthlong winter break between terms at Graceland, she would take a small group of students to Haiti, to teach health principles to village women there. Babies were dying of diarrhea, and the group taught the women how to make a mixture of sugar, salt, and clean water that served as oral rehydration therapy. She went on similar trips to the Dominican Republic and Jamaica and then Africa and beyond, enlisting community health workers to continue her work after she left.

Kirkpatrick admits she didn't always know at first what she was doing: "I made huge mistakes with the Haitians, bless their hearts. They were so patient with me." But several years later, the Africans benefited.

From the beginning she enlisted a group of community volunteers and gave them questionnaires that asked: "What is the biggest threat to your children's health? What is the biggest threat to your health?" The answers were different depending on the village, but she refined and adapted them based on the template she had created in Haiti. Many of these original health workers are still working with her today.

Even while holding down a full-time job and raising two children, Kirkpatrick continued to educate village women by using her vacation time to travel to developing countries. Her husband had left NASA to take a job in international development, focusing on Africa, and he helped her gain access to villages there.

She describes herself as losing her heart in the little village of Chiba, Zaire (now the Democratic Republic of the Congo) in the late 1980s while training the villagers there. There the biggest threat to children's health was leg ulcers. At first, when the children came to her, and she could see the bones and tendons in the craters in their legs, she thought this was beyond her ability to treat.

But the villagers were insistent, "So I did some research and came up with guava leaves. You just pick them off the tree and you wash them. And then you boil them like you would a cup of tea. You cool them and strain them and use them like an antiseptic to clean wounds and it works wonderfully." She also encouraged the villagers to begin growing peanuts, which provide nutritional protection against the ulcers. The leg ulcers disappeared in less than a year. Today, she said, the older people in the village barely remember that they were once a scourge. Once that problem was solved, she and the community workers moved on to reducing the maternal death rate, and she was able to expand those efforts to Zambia and Malawi.

Kirkpatrick's experiences across decades slowly coalesced into her

Big Thing: HealthEd Connect, which provides health and education programs to tens of thousands of children and adults around the world. She can't imagine having started her nonprofit when she was in her thirties. "Without question I couldn't do what I'm doing with this program if hadn't done all the previous things," she told me.

All of her previous experiences, combined with her academic and professional connections, layered on top of each other over time and enabled her to start her company. After her time as dean of nursing she served for three years as the director of development for fund-raising at Graceland University, and the skills she learned in that role helped her raise money for her new venture.

Kirkpatrick and her husband are deeply involved in the Community of Christ, but she says she is not an evangelizer. She does consider her work to be a calling, and of her eventual path in life, she said, "I was called in this direction but didn't know it."

To others who have a dream like hers but not enough time to pursue it she says: "Anything you have a passion for can be done as a hobby. It doesn't have to be a full-time endeavor. I'd start as a hobby and follow that passion."

Marc Freedman is founder and CEO of Encore.org, which aims to help people in midlife and beyond accomplish big projects that benefit society. Its Purpose Prize has been called a kind of MacArthur genius grant for retirees. I asked Freedman, Is there something about this time in life that makes people want to focus on the greater good? Yes, he said. Part of it is that they suddenly realize that they can't take time for granted in the way that they did when they were twenty or thirty. At the same time, they have acquired a sizable store of know-how and experience. And although death is closer than it ever was, there is still plenty of time in life to think about making an impact and leaving a legacy.

Freedman is interested in the work of David W. Galenson, an

economics professor at the University of Chicago who has identified two casts of mind—conceptual and incremental—that tend to flower at different stages of life. The work of conceptual artists is bold, precise, certain, and carefully planned. By contrast, experimental types are vague, uncertain, intuitive, and incremental. They progress through trial and error, and that takes time.

Galenson examines this dichotomy mainly in relation to artists, but his research applies to many kinds of creators, including people like Sherri Kirkpatrick. Think how different her path was compared with Silicon Valley whiz kids like Mark Zuckerberg and Steve Jobs, whose very youth and lack of experience helped them imagine new possibilities.

Almost all the winners of the Purpose Prize are accidental, incremental entrepreneurs, Freedman said, finding their way to their projects based on a lifetime of accumulated experience. For example, there was Catalino Tapia, a gardener who came to California from Mexico with a sixth-grade education and almost no money, and managed to put his son through college. Decades later, he created a program that enabled other people like him to do the same. He was awarded the prize at age sixty-four.

Cézanne was the artistic equivalent of these incremental entrepreneurs. He rarely signed his works because he never considered them to be finished. Picasso, by contrast, was conceptual. "Picasso's certainty about his art contrasted sharply with Cézanne's doubt," Galenson writes in his book *Old Masters and Young Geniuses*. Cézanne destroyed many of his paintings because they didn't rise to the ideal in his mind. Picasso, by contrast, signed and dated all of his paintings. He was done.

Picasso managed to radically change his style several times in his life. This is rare for the conceptual artist, who tends to peak early. Radical conceptual innovation "depends on the ability to perceive and appreciate the value of extreme deviations from existing conventions," Galenson says, "and this ability will tend to decline with experience, as habits of thought become more firmly established." Experimental artists benefit from an accumulation of experience, whereas a "growing awareness of the complexity of their disciplines" works against the conceptual innovator.

For conceptual artists, experience is a drawback because it can hinder the bolt-out-of-the-blue insight. Why do we have to do things *that* way? No reason, except they have always been done that way.

Galenson uses critics' judgments, art history books, and auction prices to establish a kind of quality gauge for artists' works. How old were various artists when they created their most significant work? Interestingly, the artists who peaked earlier (the outlier Picasso being a big exception) tended to be one-hit conceptual wonders, famous for helping to start some new movement. Some artists who peaked later did not have a single work represented in an art history book, but were commonly acknowledged to be among the greatest of their era; it was their body of work rather than a single work that led to this assessment.

Galenson demonstrates that the conceptual/experimental division can be extended to other artistic domains. "As is the case in painting, important conceptual sculptors, poets, novelists and movie directors tend to make their greatest contributions suddenly and early in their careers, whereas their experimental counterparts innovate gradually and arrive at their greatest achievements late in their careers."

I couldn't help wondering where Autumn de Forest fits into this dichotomy, if at all. Her artistic bent seems more intuitive than conceptual. Her Barbie Marilyn "riff" on Warhol, who was a conceptual artist, is experimental. Hers is a rare combination.

In most cases, the success of an artist depends on external evaluation. If a parent or a teacher or a mentor recognizes that a child has talent in a particular area, it can make all the difference, as it did with Autumn. In areas such as math and science, training is crucial to achieving a Big Thing. In the arts, it may be possible to move forward without adult support, but it would take an unusually resilient and determined young person to make that happen.

In *From Bauhaus to Our House* Tom Wolfe imagines "some young lad who could take a piece of marble and carve a pillow that looks so full of voluptuous downy billows that you would have willingly buried your head in it" being drawn to the prestigious art program at Yale University in the 1950s and there encountering the fine arts program of the abstract artist Josef Albers, who asked his students to "start from zero," working with simple squares of colored paper. This "reincarnation of Bernini" would have had trouble finding his way in an environment so utterly at odds with his natural bent. Whose works have we lost because of such mismatches?

In the formative years the presence or absence of role models in one's domain can influence future creativity, although Teresa Amabile notes that "lesser thinkers require role models more than major thinkers do."

How can a parent clear the right creative path on behalf of a talented child? How can a creative adolescent or young adult, alternately wanting to rebel and conform, set the gauge just right? How can an adult, dealing with multiple commitments and loved ones who may or may not understand one's creative yearnings, know which direction to take? As important as outside evaluation is, internal evaluation is even more crucial a gauge. In my own experience, and in hearing the stories of others, it's clear that intrinsic motivation should be the predominant guiding force as one struggles to find an answer.

There is a gender divide in this area. Looking at history, it's safe to say that men are much more comfortable overturning the established creative order. Men such as Picasso and Braque reveled in shocking the art world by introducing the bold, primitive forms of cubism. Women, raised to comfort and appease, may be more hesitant to pursue nonconformist creative ideas. Their path may be more incremental, and they may bloom later. I am reminded of Louise

Bourgeois, who lived in the shadow of her artist husband until her eighties, when she burst onto the scene with her mammoth and intimidating spider sculptures. (Interestingly, her work derives from her childhood—the spiders are a representation of her mother—but it is a childhood informed by seven decades of memories and interpretations.)

In his study of creativity, Howard Gardner found a ten-year rule at work: "At least ten years of steady work at a discipline of craft seem required before that métier has been mastered." Future breakthroughs may or may not occur after that. In short, it's a long, hard slog without any guarantees. Similarly, Malcolm Gladwell has written that achieving expertise in any area requires ten thousand hours of practice.

But wait, there's a loophole as far as I'm concerned: Did I ever say that a Big Thing had to be a work of genius, a breakthrough, or even good? No! That would be nice, but I'm saying that whatever your age, it may be good for you to complete a big, meaningful project because it's good for your brain.

"The hardware of the brain is far from fixed at birth," the psychiatrist and researcher Jeffrey Schwartz writes in his book *The Mind and the Brain.* "Instead, it is dynamic and malleable." It's true that the brain is at its most plastic in the younger years, but the adult brain is like an ongoing construction site, and the way we use it can result in "the wholesale remapping of neural real estate," he writes.

Even the elderly can alter the inner workings of their brains by taking on challenging projects, Schwartz told me in an interview: yes, some reduction in capacity is inevitable, but look at people like the historian and philosopher Jacques Barzun, who was still writing books into his nineties. Among the elderly, limitations are probably much more fluid than we once thought, he said.

"Working on a big creative project is the kind of constructive, goal-oriented attention that rewires the brain in adaptive ways," he said. "You're going to be in the process of forming and realizing your true self." So even if your Big Thing turns out to be a big misshapen mess, and the outside world ignores or even ridicules it (not that you ever have to show it to them), it may still be worth doing.

When I visited Dr. Jim Levine of the Mayo Clinic for this book, he wondered if anyone would ever deliberately try to do a bad Big Thing. Yes, he concluded, they might, because of the benefits of neuroplasticity. (And, he added, they might meet some interesting people along the way.)

But what is it that leads some people to complete Big Things, while others never try and still others try and fail? Regardless of where they are in the life cycle, Schwartz said, "the whole issue of persistence is huge. I think it has as much to do with motivation as anything else."

"How's this?" Schwartz said. "Winners never quit, and quitters never win." And then it came to this: Dr. Schwartz, a professor at the University of California, Los Angeles, and an expert in neuroplasticity, cited *The Little Engine That Could.*

Call it striving, resilience, willpower. The word *grit* has made its way into the academic and pop psychology lexicon to try to explain this quality that causes some people to succeed despite serious disadvantages. It's that make-or-break quality that gets people over to the other side, from repose to exertion. Though Schwartz is an academic researcher, he does not believe this quality can really be measured. Some neuroscientists just can't deal with the fact that resilience arises from something that is nonmaterial. It is ineffable.

I asked Schwartz whether older people could develop grit if they've never had it before. It sounds odd to use the word *grit* in a geriatric sense, he said—it's more commonly used in connection with adolescence.

That got me thinking: maybe by the time you are older, grit becomes generativity—the word that the psychologist Erik Erikson used to describe a state that older people can reach if they do not sink into stagnation and "rejectivity." As awareness of one's mortality takes hold, the self-absorption of adolescence and early adulthood wanes and one begins to be concerned with giving back to succeeding generations.

The resolve of generativity can produce beautiful and lasting things. I heard that resolve in Linval Thomas, who had faith that he would one day record a reggae album even as his life diverged away from the goal for decades. I heard it in Sherri Kirkpatrick, who didn't fully realize her dreams until she was sixty-five but slowly built up to them throughout her adult life. I saw that resolve at the American Visionary Art Museum in the form of complex creations that were the capstones of deep and eccentrically lived lives.

I have to say, though, I heard some of that spirit in Autumn de Forest, age thirteen, who earnestly told me that she continues to want to change the world through her art. That purity of heart can emerge at any age.

EIGHT

The Big Thing and Your Day Job

The fact that you already have a full-time job may not be a good enough reason to delay working on your Big Thing. You really need to stop and determine whether you are pulling one over on yourself with that well-worn excuse.

Consider the following examples of people who managed to thrive creatively while holding down day jobs. Some needed the jobs for the money, and some didn't. Some of the jobs were in similar fields as their creative work, some in completely different ones.

Franz Kafka worked full-time for an insurance company and wrote at night in his cramped apartment when the rest of his family was asleep. He had wanted to find a job that demanded as little as possible of his time and energy, but through overconscientiousness wound up taking his work more to heart than he had planned.

But that was not all bad. "Kafka's job, while imposing an onerous routine, also provided a structure and status on which he came to depend for a large measure of identity and self-respect," his biographer Ernst Pawel writes. His job also gave him firsthand exposure to the mindless bureaucracy that he explored with such brilliance in *The Trial* and *The Castle*.

For some reason, the insurance industry has attracted other creative giants. The poet Wallace Stevens worked at the Hartford Accident and Indemnity Company from the age of thirty-six until his death. "I find that having a job is one of the best things in the world that could happen to me," he said. "It introduces discipline and regularity into one's life." It also meant he didn't have to worry about money. The composer Charles Ives was also a high-earning executive in the insurance industry.

Albert Einstein worked in the Swiss Patent Office while coming up with the theory of relativity. The poet William Carlos Williams was a medical doctor. Joseph Heller worked in advertising. The list goes on.

Where did they find the time? Often by establishing a routine and also by exploiting the interstices in their lives. Anthony Trollope, author of forty-seven novels, wrote for three hours in the morning, starting at five thirty, while also holding down a demanding job as a surveyor for the post office. He had to travel extensively by rail for his job and at first spent that time reading, "but if I intended to make a profitable business out of my writing, and, at the same time, do my best for the Post Office, I must turn these hours more to account," he wrote in his autobiography. He wrote most of *Barchester Towers* on the train: "My only objection to the practice came from the appearance of literary ostentation, to which I felt myself subject when going to work before four or five fellow passengers."

Trollope was no slouch at his day job. He worked hard to improve mail efficiency wherever he traveled or was stationed, and is credited with introducing the freestanding postbox to Britain.

Still, it would be nice not to have to work. Think of how much time you could spend on what really matters.

Then again, maybe not.

I finally started writing a book for real when I had a full-time job. Over and over, I heard from people that constraints were important to getting a Big Thing done. My day job performed that service for me. In my mind I saw the open spots in my day and my week, and I knew I had to work on the book during some of those times. Time constraints gave me energy and focus.

There were drawbacks, though. In the morning I got up and wrote words, and when I went to work I edited and wrote words, and sometimes I had to write my own words for work and then go home and write words or read them for the book. Words, words, words—it was too much!

At the same time, I had never written a nonfiction book before, and it was much harder and different than writing or editing an article. Some of my editorial work for the *Times* had been off-loaded to my brain's habit circuits, but that was not the case for writing a book.

As research has shown, we only have a limited amount of willpower, and it becomes depleted whether we use it on our day job or our Big Thing, or something else like family responsibilities. When I worked on the book for two hours in the morning, I could get things done at my job if they were not too demanding. But if I had a particularly challenging day at the office—if I had to write an article or seriously rework a long article I was editing—I could feel my productivity suffer. Similarly, if I hadn't written at all in the morning (which was common enough) I seldom made up for it in the evening if I'd had a strenuous day at work.

As the final deadline approached, I was able to take one month off from my job—two weeks' leave and two weeks' vacation—to work solely on this book. I felt I needed a break from living so intensely in two worlds at once.

I had an image of how this would play out. I would get up, have my coffee, write or do interviews for two hours, take a lunch break, work for one hour, take a nap, then work for one more hour, and take the evening off as a reward. That seemed like a reasonable schedule that even I could follow. That, however, is not what happened.

It's true that I did get up every morning and have my coffee, and I did take a nap almost every afternoon. And if I had made commitments to call or meet people, of course I followed through on those. But otherwise I almost never started working until about seven in the evening, and then I worked for two or maybe three hours. Before then I did things like read mysteries, watch *The Young and the Restless* after a ten-year hiatus (Victor was still up to his tricks), pace around the apartment, drink wine at 1 p.m., and go out for a late lunch or an early dinner.

So given my druthers, I learned, I prefer to work in the evening. It's what I had already tended to do on the weekends. Nightfall, apparently, is a kind of deadline enforcer for me. I did get somewhat more work done when I was on my leave—and I had much more energy at night after a day spent lollygagging instead of working in the office. But the huge wads of time I now had oppressed me— more time to be lazy meant more time to feel guilty, too. By the end of my weeks off, I was craving the structure of the office. It was actually a relief to return to work and see that I had just a limited time in the morning, a limited time at night, and the weekends, to get my work done.

For some people, a career itself is their Big Thing. A job is so satisfying and challenging that there is no psychic yearning to take on a side project.

For others, it's best to take a job that is not too intellectually taxing so as to free up energy for the projects that really matter. That is what the composer Philip Glass did. He came from a family of modest means in Baltimore and could not afford to work full-time on his music until he was forty-one. When he first arrived in New York in the 1950s to study at the Juilliard School, he got a job loading trucks for Yale Trucking in Manhattan; he worked five hours a day, five days a week, from 3 to 8 p.m. From 10 a.m. to 1 p.m. he would do the following, according to his memoir *Words Without Music*: "I set a clock on the piano, put some music paper on the table nearby, and sat at the piano from ten until one. It didn't matter whether I composed a note of music or not. The other part of the exercise was that I didn't write music at any other time of the day or night. The strategy was to tame my muse, encouraging it to be active at the times I had set and at no other times." The first week was brutal, but after a short while, "I started writing music, just to have something to do."

It took him nearly two months to become comfortable with his new rule, but gradually "the habit of attention became available to me, and that brought real order to my life." In addition, "I was never tempted to compose outside of times I set for myself." He persisted in this habit for more than four decades. Only recently has he allowed himself to do some unscheduled work again.

In the mid-1970s, when Glass was married and had children, he worked as a cabdriver. "The passengers could be exasperating—the variety of people and the outrageous kinds of behavior that happen in taxis are known only to people who have to spend a hundred miles a night in a taxicab three or four times a week. The good thing was I didn't have to work that many hours, because in three or four nights I could make enough money to live on." Much of his famous opera *Einstein on the Beach* was written at night, after his taxi shift.

When I was in my twenties, I nursed my goal of writing a book, and I thought that an undemanding job was the answer. After I graduated from college with a degree in journalism, I did not take the recommended, dues-paying career route of getting a job at a small to medium-size newspaper like the *New Haven Register* or the *Saginaw News*. The fact that I had graduated into a job-killing recession made it easier to stay in the part-time job I had held in college, as a customer service representative for the circulation department of the *Minneapolis Star Tribune*. But I questioned my decision while performing the internal calculus that so many people do, involving pay, skill, market realities, creative aspirations, and self-appraisal.

I worked twenty-four hours a week, evenings and weekends, and I did some freelancing for local publications. I lived in a studio apartment where the rent was $275 a month. According to the Social Security statement I recently received, I made $7,700 in 1984.

Nowadays, people in Bangalore do these kinds of jobs, but back then it was an all-local workforce. Mainly the job involved taking calls from customers who hadn't received their papers and sending out a replacement or crediting their account. A mildly unpleasant crackly noise in my earpiece would signal a call, at which point I would say "Circulation, Phyllis Cleary" (we were allowed to use pseudonyms in case angry non-paper-receiving customers decided to come after us).

"Hello, we didn't get our paper," 60 percent of the customers said, and the actions I needed to take were limited and predictable. The only variable was the caller's emotional tone. Most were polite or mildly querulous. But self-righteous, ballistic anger (probably signaling deeper issues at home or a truly abysmal carrier) did occasionally erupt.

On a Sunday in January after a snowstorm, we would take calls nonstop. But on a beautiful evening in June, sometimes twenty or thirty minutes would go by without a call. There was no requirement to do anything else, and I read huge sections of *Moby-Dick* while at work.

On Mondays and Wednesdays, my days off, I remember feeling as if the days stretched out like long, clean carpets. I would walk around Lake of the Isles and vow to spend the rest of the day on my novel. But that would have meant actually starting my novel, which I never did do. I think I recognized that I wasn't yet old enough to have much of substance to write, but that didn't stop me from berating myself for being lazy.

John Kuchera, who lives in the Morningside Heights neighborhood of Manhattan, went through something similar when he was in his twenties. After Kuchera graduated from high school, he and a friend bought an apartment complex in Rochester, New York, sold it, and made a big profit. Kuchera bought a house in Maine and decided to write the Great American Novel. He got as far as his name and the first sentence. He just didn't have anything to say yet. Now, at fifty-two, he has much less money and many more stories—and a Big Thing he is working on, small step by small step.

In his day job, Kuchera is a full-time janitor for Columbia University. In his off hours he founded the Kuchera Museum, which is devoted to the paintings of his late father, also named John.

I explained to Kuchera that I was looking for a blue-collar worker for my chapter about day jobs, and he said, "Well, that's me." When I met him at his apartment, he was literally wearing a shirt with a blue collar, along with some plaid shorts.

Kuchera was born in Cleveland and grew up in Rochester, where his father designed cards (the long, skinny, highbrow ones) for American Greetings; he worked with Tom Wilson, creator of the *Ziggy* comic strip. John Sr. later became a designer for the Young & Rubicam ad agency, and then Leo Burnett in Chicago. Always, during his working life, and after he retired and moved back to Rochester, his father would paint, often with oil or acrylic on fiberboard or cardboard. His paintings are a form of folk art that reflect his Slovakian background, with bright bold colors, frequently featuring angels, peasant women, birds, and cats.

A love of art runs in the family: John Jr. and his two sisters all paint, too. In the 1980s, John Jr. moved to Manhattan, where his sisters went to art school, and he took art classes when he could. He got married, had a daughter, and worked various printing jobs while painting in his spare time.

Kuchera said he and his first wife outgrew each other, and after their divorce he eventually married Claire Cooper, a songwriter and pianist. When Cooper's mother died, she left her enough money so they could buy the apartment in Morningside Heights. By then Kuchera was working at a print shop in New Jersey and became tired of the reverse commute. So one day he left his apartment and thought, "Let me walk ten minutes in every direction and see what kind of job I can find." It so happened that the employment office for Columbia University was within that radius, and that's how he ended up working there, first in catering, and now as a janitor for a faculty apartment building.

Kuchera works from 7 a.m. to 4 p.m. and has a great commute. "I walk down Broadway, and I walk right past Grant's Tomb and Riverside Church. On Riverside Church there's an angel blowing a trumpet. So every morning I kind of wave to her and say hi. So that starts my day."

During his workday, he cleans the floors, the windows, and the railings. He also cleans the roof—"you'd be surprised how much crap gets up there." He takes out the trash. In the winter he shovels. When there isn't snow he cleans the sidewalk with a hose, a blower, or a broom. In the warmer months, a highlight of his day is watering the flowers out front. He also likes cleaning the brass in the lobby and seeing the sun shine on it. He delivers packages to the tenants. He's a hearty, extroverted man. He likes to say good morning to the tenants and chat with them about various and sundry topics.

Sometimes it's busy at work—say, contractors might leave a big mess—sometimes it's quiet. But regardless, Kuchera always gets two fifteen-minute breaks and an hour for lunch. It's a union job and the pay is decent. He doesn't mind, and even likes the work, and he's glad to have a steady job with benefits.

Kuchera never takes his work home with him, and that has given him more energy for the Kuchera Museum, which he started in 2014 a few years after his father passed away and left behind hundreds of paintings, drawings, and comics in storage in Rochester. "I thought, What the hell am I going to do with all this stuff?" his son recalled. And then it came to him: "I'll make a museum."

Kuchera couldn't afford to rent gallery space, so the museum is in his small apartment. It's an official museum: it has nonprofit status, and he belongs to the Small Museum Alliance.

The setting is cramped but intimate. As he does with all museum visitors, Kuchera served me wine and cheese, talked about his father, and showed me his paintings. They were stacked, unframed, eight to ten or more deep on the floor and on easels, and Kuchera showed them to me one by one. There wasn't room to frame them all in the small apartment, along with art by Kuchera himself, his sisters, and his friends.

It was certainly the most intimate museum experience I have ever had, but I was a little worried about the safety of the paintings, and Kuchera admitted that he stubs his toe on them once in a while. And this collection was just the tip of the iceberg; several hundred more artworks were in storage.

As adorably quirky as the museum is, it's just not viable for Kuchera to keep it in his home indefinitely. The paintings need to be framed and archived, placed on walls and rotated. So his next Big Thing is to find a new place for it and hire a manager to oversee it. Kuchera was in the process of trying to find the right format for it and then the right funding.

"Money's no good unless you have a plan," he said. "I need a plan for the Kuchera Museum." Every week he works the angles, writing letters to various arts organizations about possible options for housing the museum, and he hopes someday that his incremental work will result in a gallery. He knows he has a tendency to think big—too big—so he wants to go slow with his goal so he gets it right.

"Time goes really quickly, but you have to wait and do it the right way," he said. "All the successful people, they did it the right way." So he's going to wait and let his plan gestate for a while. Meanwhile, he is continuing with his own painting.

Ultimately, he said, he'd like to have a gallery-size museum with rotating shows, and maybe expand beyond his father's art to put on shows featuring families like his, with multiple members who are artists.

A lot of blue-collar people work on creative projects in their off hours, Kuchera said. In fact, his union was about to hold an art show of works by its members, who are all building service workers.

Many of those workers are immigrants. In New York, we interact daily with workers who are from all over the world: the taxi driver from Pakistan, the food deliveryman from China, the cashier from Korea, the salon worker from Mexico. They all have stories, and something bigger they aspire to—maybe a Big Thing.

*　　*　　*

Cenia Paredes, from the Dominican Republic, worked for ten years at a shoe store at a mall in Jersey City, while never giving up on her goal of starting her own clothing line.

Paredes grew up in a rural village in the middle of the DR. All of her family sewed for a living. Her mother was the village seamstress: "People at the time didn't really go to a store and buy clothes—they had it custom made," Paredes said. She grew up surrounded by the sounds of sewing machines and the sight of villagers coming in for their fittings.

Her mother and father separated and eventually divorced, and Cenia and her two sisters moved in with her great-grandparents, with the mother and daughters sharing one bedroom: "It was pretty humble, but we were very happy." Her mother would sew identical outfits for the three sisters and style their hair for church on Sunday.

When her mother was cutting fabric during the day, seven-year-old Cenia would stand next to her and besiege her with questions. She would pick up scraps of cloth and try to make little pieces of her own. At the same time, she developed a passion for drawing clothes.

Her great-grandparents didn't have a television, so Cenia would go next door and watch Mexican soap operas. Seeing the elegant costumes worn by the actresses, she decided she wanted to make clothes like that someday.

By the time she was nine, she had made hundreds of fashion sketches. One of her aunts saw them and said, "Cenia, you're going to be a fashion designer like Oscar de la Renta." She had never heard of de la Renta before and said, "You can make a living designing clothes?" From that day, she decided that that was what she was going to do.

Her mother eventually married an American citizen she met in the DR and moved with him to New Jersey. A few years after Paredes had finished high school and learned English, Cenia moved to Jersey

City near her mother. She started college in Jersey City (the first in her extended family to go) but stopped after two years when she got married and quickly became pregnant with a son. Her husband, who was from the DR, was very traditional and wanted her to stay home, but because finances were tight, she got the part-time job at the shoe store. Two years later, after being promoted to store manager, she had a daughter.

The marriage went downhill, and the two divorced after five years. Paredes's dream of becoming a fashion designer had been obscured, but not extinguished. She enrolled at the Fashion Institute of Technology while continuing to work at the shoe store. Her mother helped take care of the children. (She could never have gotten where she is today without her mother, she readily admits.)

After she finished school at FIT, she began working as an assistant and then an associate designer for companies including Warnaco and Izod. Much of the work was technical and not very creative. She felt it would be very hard to climb the ladder and become a full-fledged designer at these companies—for one thing because she had children and couldn't work the endless hours required onsite.

Her mother had always taught her that if you work toward your dream, doors can open. So in 2009, remarried and with another child and while still working full-time, Paredes began creating her own collection at night and on weekends. She would work all day at her job, come home and cook dinner for the kids, and help them with their homework. Then, at nine thirty, she would work on her collection, often till two in the morning.

"You didn't get enough sleep, did you?" I said.

"No," she said. "And I'm the type of person who needs at least eight hours. I'd be beat in the morning."

But, she said, "I was very committed. For some reason I thought, This is going to be my future and I'm going to make it. I felt it in my guts." Moreover, working on her own designs did not really feel like work. She would get carried away and lose track of time. Finally, she saved up money from her day job and produced a collection of about fifteen dresses.

Finding a showroom and boutiques to sell them proved difficult in 2008, just as the market crashed. But two years later she got a break: she was one of four winners of a clothing design contest sponsored by Macy's. The contest, although it didn't come with a monetary award, enabled her to sell her clothes at Macy's, and the Macy's name gave her instant exposure and opened all kinds of doors for her.

Paredes was able to quit her day job in 2010. As an entrepreneur she has experienced some financial traumas, including a business partnership that went sour. But when I talked to her in her bright, airy seventh-floor studio on Broadway in the Garment District, she appeared to be thriving. Shortly after I spoke with her, she moved her company a few blocks away, to the showroom of a manufacturer with whom she made a licensing agreement, that led to a deal for her clothes to be sold on the Home Shopping Network and similar shopping networks in Europe and Russia. Part of her appeal is that she includes dresses for curvier women—the average American woman is a size 14, after all—and they are sexy without being vulgar, with panels that help cinch and accentuate the right parts.

I wondered how Paredes's children felt about her entrepreneurial path. "They were resentful at one point when they were teenagers because I was so focused on my business. But now they tell me that they understand that this is my passion and my dream." Also, she said, she wanted to provide them with a financial foundation. "I don't want them to start from scratch like me."

Most of the people I talked to for this book had other jobs while they pursued their Big Things, at least part of the time or at first. Over and over, I heard from them how it could be done. But finances inevitably affected the arc of their endeavors.

Sherri Kirkpatrick could not fully realize her dream of starting a nonprofit until after she retired. But she worked toward her goal during her vacations, and gained valuable knowledge and connections in the process. Ann Bancroft asked for a leave of absence from her teaching job to prepare for a polar expedition. She eventually left teaching to pursue expeditions full-time, but that came with the onerous responsibility of finding sponsors and donors. Money always enters into the equation.

In the 1980s, a book called *Do What You Love, the Money Will Follow* came out. I bought it and half pooh-poohed it while my heart couldn't help leaping at the possibility that maybe I really could be a novelist, and the money would follow! Books are written to this day that urge people to pursue their passion over a soul-deadening job. Depending on who is doing the reading, these books may be right, but in other cases they are dead wrong.

Barbara Safani, a career coach based in New York, has an obligation to help people be realistic about their creative aspirations. She's not a big believer in do what you love, the money will follow. Friends of someone who has been laid off will sometimes encourage this line of thinking because they want the person to feel good about themselves, she said, but it's generally not wise to follow your passion full bore when you feel stressed financially. Sometimes it's best to secure full-time employment while taking smaller steps toward a big dream.

If someone has always wanted to start their own business, a layoff could be the time to try it, especially if there is a good severance package. Again, well-intentioned friends may stoke that dream. But often, Safani said, people thinking of these types of transitions talk about what they love doing while not paying enough attention to the other aspects of a business. Let's say you love making jewelry and you want to start a business selling it. "There's still the aspect of creating a business and doing your bookkeeping and doing your sales. There are all these other pieces that are part of running the business that have nothing to do with your love of the particular activity, but are equally important to your success." Can you learn to enjoy or at least tolerate doing them, or find a way to outsource them?

Safani also has clients—lawyers especially—who hate their jobs and just want to up and quit to start a business. In this case a spouse concerned about financial security may not have faith in that dream and try to put the brakes on it, damaging the relationship.

Again, Safani tries to find ways for her clients to ease into a new direction, so that they have time and a financial cushion to handle some initial failures, which are pretty much inevitable. It has been gratifying, she said, to see clients who are unsure of themselves at first slowly come into their own and make a success of a small business—sometimes out of choice, after quitting a job, other times out of necessity, after being laid off.

Nancy Molitor, the clinical psychologist based in Chicago whom I mentioned in Chapter 1, is seeing more people start a creative venture early in their adult lives, maybe after saving money from a conventional job for a few years, and before they have to worry about children and a mortgage. In her generation, that was much less common, said Molitor, who is sixty. "A lot of millennials and Gen Xers are not waiting. I think the recession certainly opened their eyes to the reality that nothing is given. They don't have pensions. They aren't used to the notion that they're going to have that nest egg. They've been brought up very differently."

More of her clients, especially women, are also taking a creative risk after a life crisis such as an illness or a divorce. A woman might say: I don't want that big house I got in the divorce settlement; I'm going to sell it and open a store. "They could be thirty, they could be sixty, but they've gone through something really difficult and they've survived and they've gained strength from it."

Like Safani, she urges people to be realistic and avoid all-or-nothing behavior, such as suddenly quitting a full-time job to start a business, or, conversely, giving up entirely on a creative dream. She helps people do an honest accounting of their time—especially their screen time—and helps them find extra hours in their day to work on their Big Things.

One person who could teach others about finding—and cherishing—extra hours is forty-two-year-old Camilla Webster, a founder of New York Natives, a media company that focuses on the New York experience, especially the arts. In addition to being a busy entrepreneur, Webster is also an artist, but it took her a while to come out and say that. One of the biggest commitments she ever made was to add "artist" to her LinkedIn profile, alongside journalist, author, investor, and entrepreneur, she said.

I talked to Webster in the home where she was raised as an only child, a spacious apartment in Manhattan's East Sixties. She was educated nearby at the prestigious Brearley School for girls, and was taught early that anything was possible if you worked hard enough. Her late mother was an editor for Time Life Books, and her father was an entrepreneur who had his ups and downs. When she was fourteen, the apartment we were sitting in was ruined in a fire, and although she wasn't home at the time, that event shook her to her core. "For a long time I always believed I was not going to live to a very ripe old age," she said. "I think I saw the fragility of life very young."

She was a prolific painter when she was a child, and her parents were supportive of her going to art school and becoming an artist. But she decided it would be safer to become a journalist (although she laughs at that idea now, given the traumatic shifts that field has undergone).

After getting a master's degree in art history at St. Andrews University in Scotland, she became a radio and TV producer, working for CBS and Fox News and traveling all over the world. At Fox she covered the war on terror and was in charge of the embedded units in Iraq. Then she became a business journalist, working as an editor for the *Wall Street Journal* and on video productions for MarketWatch and Forbes as media companies began investing in the Internet. At Forbes, she interviewed CEOs and world leaders, and she used the opportunity to ask if she could see their art collections, revitalizing her interest in art.

Once in a while, when she worked as a journalist, she would paint, but that was rare. "It was almost too painful to do because it was the thing I had chosen not to do," she said.

In 2010, she left Forbes to write, along with Carol Pepper, a book called *The Seven Pearls of Financial Wisdom: A Woman's Guide to Enjoying Wealth and Power*. She knew of many women who were supporting or outearning their husbands or partners and felt society was experiencing a historic transfer of wealth to women, who might not be prepared for the responsibility. Drawing partly on her own experience, she wanted to leave a legacy to women as they came into their wealth, and to protect them from "wealth building killers," such as an unspoken assumption that they must support their extended family.

The book was published in 2012, and between promoting it and doing speaking engagements and interviews, she became exhausted. She also missed the artistic flame that had begun to flare again at Forbes.

Then her friend Laura Hill called and asked her if she could work with her on a blog called New York Natives (the precursor to the website and media company). She signed on and enjoyed an opportunity to be funky and creative for a change. As the blog evolved into a startup she felt the desire to paint again: "There was this hunger in me to be creative, to be around artistic people, to be around paintings. And it was deep and loud." She painted a series of flowers and realized, "There's that talent, what you used to do. It's there."

"So having a job that was similar sparked that," I said, and I was a little surprised because startups are known for devouring all your time.

Yes, she said. New York Natives reawakened her to the culture that was all around her and pulled her in the direction of the Art Students League, where she became a student of the painter Pat Lipsky, who was a breakthrough female artist in the 1960s. "She was hugely encouraging, hugely understanding of my schedule," Webster said. "I would come when I could."

Then New York Natives hired a CEO and an editor in chief, and Webster was able to take time off from the startup to attend a deep immersion summer school. She came back from that with a sizable body of work and used it to secure coveted studio space at the Mana Contemporary complex in Jersey City. She returned to the startup and also worked on her art at the studio. She was there for seven months and had recently had a showing of her paintings and photographs in her home. Webster had amassed about six hundred photographs and forty paintings to her name after just two years.

"How much sleep do you get?" I asked her, wondering if she was another one of those short sleepers.

"I sleep from eleven to five fifty."

"That's pretty exact!"

She said that despite her busy schedule, "I'm rigorous about the boundaries around my sleep."

With all her responsibilities, it can be very hard to fit in her painting, but she does it with the help of her family and colleagues. It's important to get your believers around you, she said.

In a video talk for TEDx (an independent outgrowth of the well-known TED Talks), she urges people to "decelerate" and live in the present through art. In her own life, she says, decelerating has enabled her to turn around and "accelerate with purpose."

Some of her paintings are big and the work is very physical. As she stands up and applies the oil in layers, the motion of the brushwork can turn into a kind of physical meditation for her. She created a series of what she calls meditation paintings. They are soft, colorful, layered, undulating, and meant to produce feelings of calm and joy. Her photographs—often of street art and murals or even just an unusual shape formed by cracks on the sidewalk—are intended to show the beauty and unexpected artistry of everyday life.

Gradually, her abstract images began to expand into real images of people, places, and things, some of them reflecting her perspectives on war and suffering.

One of her more figurative paintings is called *Tough Job*, which depicts a group of uniformed men she saw working laundry jobs at Dukes Hotel in London. She found out that they were from Eastern Europe, and they would come to London for nine months, usually with just a backpack, and send their wages home. "They were very handsome men who fit into this very elegant atmosphere, but actually a very challenging life story was going on in the background." There was a humble heroism in their story, she said.

To me and others who are trying to complete Big Things while also working, she said: Don't work on the hard part when you want to do the fun part. Do the thing first that feels the most natural and gives you the most joy.

Also, people starting on a "journey of duality," as she calls it, need to protect their commitment to their creative passion at any cost, she said. "Honor your commitment. Even if it's twenty minutes, honor that time. Put your stake in the ground" until that creative project becomes a part of your identity.

Announce your new identity in the virtual world, Webster said. Post your work on Facebook and perhaps get a website. She started becoming comfortable with her identity as an artist when she posted a few paintings to Facebook and got a positive response. It may not seem quite real at first, but then reality starts to catch up. The work starts to build on itself and resonate.

For most of us, social media is a double-edged sword. I don't need to remind you how much time you probably spend on things like Twitter and Facebook and TV and Web surfing despite working. I'm not sure how useful it will be for me to tell you to cut down on those things and work on your Big Thing instead, because this isn't just a mathematical time equation. Somewhere inside your head, a switch has to flip and this has to become a commitment, and it has to become part of your identity. Then you make the time.

No matter who you are and what you do, you probably have at least twenty minutes a day—and probably much more—to work on your project, and that adds up. You need to trust in the power of incrementalism. This is true in general with creative projects, but especially when you have a full-time job.

"I think a really important part of the equation is that I got to a place of consistently doing it, sometimes imperfectly, for over two years," Webster said, and that's what everybody who has a day (or a night) job has to accept. Chances are if you work on it a little, almost every day, you can get your Big Thing done. It won't be perfect, it might take longer than you expected, it might not be what you wanted it to be, but it will get done.

NINE

You're Not Alone

S*ome of the Big Things* I discuss here may seem at first glance to be the work of one person, but in fact they are not. *On the Origin of Species,* for one, would never have appeared in print if not for the insights and contributions of Darwin's scientist friends and the support of his wife and family.

The artist and child prodigy Autumn de Forest could not have achieved her early success without the active collaboration of her parents, who provided her with the time and materials—and even put their own careers on hold—to help cultivate her talent. Sherri Kirkpatrick, the founder of the nonprofit HealthEd Connect, has collaborated with women in countries like Haiti, Congo, and Malawi to identify the most pressing health problems in their villages and come up with realistic ways to solve them, given local beliefs and resources.

This book is a collaboration. It may be my name on the cover, but behind that name are an agent and editor, other publishing company employees, all the sources I talked to, the books I read for research, and the friends who gave me encouragement during the long, tortured process of writing it.

I came to realize that I made it a point to acquire these collaborators because I knew I would never write a book otherwise. And you may need to do that, too. That's because collaboration creates accountability.

Nice Minnesota girl that I am, I never want to let other people down. I feel guilty if I do, and according to research, guilt-prone people are less likely to collaborate in the first place because they are so afraid they will disappoint other members of the team. No wonder it took me so long to get to this point.

I have no trouble letting *myself* down, though. My failure in ear-lier years to write this book amounted to a broken promise to my future selves, who were counting on it for their happiness and fulfill-ment. You could say that a Big Thing is a collaboration between past, present, and future selves, with procrastination constantly trying to break up the relationship.

But in its traditional sense, collaboration involves two or more separate people interacting in messy real time to create a brand-new Big Thing.

One of the best—and the worst—things about collaboration is that you're in it together.

When you're working on a Big Thing, it is essential to break it into smaller parts. What makes it so hard is trying to marshal those pieces into a larger whole. Sometimes you simply can't see the whole while you are immersed in the parts. As I write this book, I must sometimes burrow myself inside an increment of it and then come up for air and try to see where—or even if—that small piece has a place in the overarching structure.

It's easy as a solo creator to feel hopeless and helpless. If no one is around to act as a goad and a sounding board, you may give up too soon—right before a big breakthrough might have emerged. A trusted collaborator can say, "No, that's not crazy, let's give it a try." Or, "Why don't you try this?"

There's a certain point in almost every creative project where "you have this feeling of being lost in the wilderness," said Parag Chordia, who has collaborated on several successful smartphone apps. Collab-orators can buck you up and help you find your way.

But things can get complicated and confusing pretty fast as humans who are parts of a whole start assembling ideas that are also parts of a whole. With the right group of people, the result is a beautiful product that somehow exceeds the sum of its parts. With the wrong people, the project is at risk of shattering into jagged pieces.

*   *   *

"When to switch between the social part and the antisocial part is a difficult choice" in creative work, said Robert Sutton, a professor of organizational behavior at Stanford University. "It depends on the task and it depends on the nature of the person."

It is no accident, he said, that Andrew Wiles came up with the proof for Fermat's last mathematical theorem, which had remained unsolved for 350 years, by working in secrecy and almost completely alone.

"I realized that anything to do with Fermat's Last Theorem generates too much interest," Wiles told the PBS program *Nova.* "You can't really focus yourself for years unless you have undivided concentration, which too many spectators would have destroyed." And yet, he eventually emerged with the proof in 1993 by building on the work of all the mathematicians who had come before him.

Why collaborate? In some cases there may not be a choice. You may not have the expertise to do a Big Thing on your own. This is often the case in science and technology, and in business and non-profit ventures. In the arts, the very nature of the domain or project may require collaboration. Theater, film, dance, and opera are necessarily more collaborative than literature, along with some types of visual art and music.

The *New York Times*, where I work, is a major collaborative enterprise. A major story may have just one or two names in the byline, but many more people have worked behind the scenes to get it published—editors, designers, videographers, graphic artists, and more.

I am an editor, and I also write articles. Although I work hard as an editor, I do feel that the stories I write are "mine," whereas the ones I edit are not mine, even if I have struggled over them. When I edit a story, I am more of a handmaiden, sewing and snipping and reconfiguring its parts but trying my best to make sure it still "belongs" to the writer.

But as an editor I may also have more influence. If I am editing a piece and the writer and I disagree, I may cite the style, standards, and precedents of the *Times* to make my case—and these are powerful. They are always fluctuating to adapt to current realities, but at their core they are a distillation of more than 160 years of collaboration.

I have often felt a great psychic satisfaction in completing a project with several collaborators. The emphasis feels just right when I don't feel as if I "own" the project and yet I am a necessary part of the whole.

Newspapers, films, and other collaborative endeavors operate according to hierarchies, some more rigid than others. Is it even possible to work in a collaborative setting without having a hierarchy? Sutton doesn't think so. He gets in trouble for this idea, he said, but "I can't find any human groups that aren't hierarchical and authoritarian." Even the Orpheus Chamber Orchestra—which famously does not have a conductor—chooses a different member to serve as a concertmaster for each musical piece, and the president has control over the programming.

"Maybe it could be two people in charge," Sutton said. "But then one of them seems to be more in charge than the other."

Parag Chordia thinks hierarchies can be divided up according to expertise. In the case of his apps, his wife, Prerna Gupta, with whom he collaborates, has been the ultimate arbiter on user-related issues. In technical areas, he is the final decider.

There's a very fine line—and often a tension—between having a leader and a clear direction, and also making sure that everyone has equal creative say, Chordia said. But in the end it's important to have a leader, he said, "because where you disagree—that's where you lose all your time."

Sutton, citing research by his Stanford colleagues Deborah Gruenfeld and Larissa Tiedens, said that collaborations suffer when there is a lack of consensus about who is in charge. People become less committed and less productive, and unhealthy competition for status emerges. Collaborative groups need to know how to fight, and leaders are crucial to shaping that process, he said. "The key is to have a contest of ideas and some sort of constructive process for either recombining them or figuring out which ones are better."

Sutton offers these suggestions in the name of making collaboration run more smoothly:

- Don't allow criticism to accompany the initial stages of idea generation. "Make it safe for people to suggest crazy or controversial ideas. After you have some ideas, then invite people to push back on them."
- Make sure everyone is included, by reining in the talkers and encouraging the quieter people to speak up.
- Monitor nonverbal behavior, and assess how it might, even unwittingly, have affected other people in the group.
- Learn which people are thin-skinned and thick-skinned, and adjust your communication style accordingly.
- After a conflict, "Soothe those who feel personally attacked and whose ideas were shot down. If anyone made personal attacks, call them on it and coach them to do otherwise."

People who self-identify as artists often have trouble working in groups and dealing with the conflicts that arise, said Kimberly Elsbach, a professor of organizational behavior at the University of California, Davis. That is what she and Francis J. Flynn, of Stanford University, discovered when they studied collaborations among a group of designers at a large toy manufacturer.

Elsbach and Flynn found that the designers could be divided into two main categories: artistic and problem solving. The artistic designers viewed themselves as individual creators. They saw their work as emerging from their own vision and wanted control of it from beginning to end. But this was not practical—they needed to work with others to make sure the final product fell within certain practical constraints, including financial ones. To achieve this they were required to collaborate not only with other designers but with people in other departments, such as marketing.

The artistic designers, they found, had no problem contributing ideas. Rather, they had trouble accepting them. Curiously, most of the research on creative collaboration has centered on idea generation, and very little on idea taking, said Elsbach, who is trying to make up for that deficit in her research.

When artistic types view big projects with a sense of personal ownership, they can see external input as a threat to their very identity, Elsbach said. The feeling is: "This isn't mine anymore." Problem solvers feel no such personal investment in a project. Their job is to improve on the ideas of others and fix the issues that keep a good idea from moving forward. They don't care about "owning" a project, although they may feel pride in their area of expertise.

If an artistic type is allowed to run roughshod over a problem solver, the result can be an impractical product that never gets past the drawing board. The two types need each other. So how to make artists more receptive to incorporating outside ideas?

In other research she has done, Elsbach has found that presenting an idea in a dispassionate tone—as if you don't really care about it—makes artistic types more likely to accept it. The more enthusiastic you sound about something, the more it seems to be part of your identity and therefore threatening to an artist's own. Another solution is to bring artistic visionaries into a project later so they don't feel that they own it, Elsbach said. They're much more amenable to helping others flesh out their ideas. And in projects where they are the leader, it's often more effective to present ideas in more general rather than specific, "x, y, z" terms, so that they are viewed more as inspirational than dictatorial, she found.

Keith Sawyer, an education professor at the University of North Carolina at Chapel Hill, uses the word *equivocality* to describe a type of indirect communication that leads to effective collaboration. He first identified this form of interaction as a pianist who performed with jazz ensembles in Chicago, and he believes it can be applied to many creative endeavors.

In a jazz improvisation, the drummer might introduce a certain rhythm pattern, which the pianist then takes up and embeds in a different musical phrase. This changes the meaning of the music even as it retains the original pattern.

The most innovative groups are the ones that constantly modify and revise their ideas in this manner, Sawyer said. "They start with one idea, and then someone thinks of a different variation on it, and a third person thinks of a totally different way of looking at it. The ideas then unfold and transform over time." In this way, the generation and evaluation of ideas are blended together.

In improvisatory collaboration, Sawyer said, it's important to make sure that a project is not about you and your ideas. "The group is not there to execute your vision," he said, although if you are a group leader you may need to gently guide it in one direction or another. "You have to step back and allow the solutions to emerge from the group dynamic." Improvisational comedy works in a similar way, he added, and taking an improv class can be a good way to let go of that "It's mine!" mind-set.

Crucial to this process is "deep listening," where other group members are genuinely open to other ideas and respond in an unplanned way. This helps usher in a state of "group flow," Sawyer says in his book *Group Genius*, drawing on the work of Mihaly Csikszentmihalyi, who defined a state of flow as being completely absorbed in creative work that stretches but does not surpass one's capabilities.

When a group, as opposed to an individual, experiences flow, a paradox is involved because "participants must feel in control, yet at the same time they must remain flexible, listen closely, and always be willing to defer to the emergent flow of the group," Sawyer writes. "The most innovative teams are the ones that can manage that paradox."

I witnessed that paradox in action when I sat in on a rehearsal of a play called *The Astonishing Times of Timothy Cratchit*, written by Allan Knee and performed by the WorkShop Theater Company in Manhattan.

The WorkShop Theater began in 1994 as an informal group where artists could test their new work through readings and modest productions. Now operating out of a building in the Garment District, the not-for-profit company holds regular readings and stagings of works in progress.

Collaboration is central to the theater's mission—and not just the usual kind that occurs among the director, actors, and other principals of a play. Playwrights here understand that the play they come in with will not be the same as the one that eventually appears onstage, as participants and observers high and low have a chance to make their mark on the script. Even audience members can "talk back" to the playwright during regular Sunday night readings of new plays, so they are collaborators as well.

Plays that germinated at the WorkShop Theater have gone on to be produced in theaters around the world. The Oscar-nominated film and Broadway musical *Finding Neverland* emerged out of a play Knee first tested and honed at the theater.

The play by Knee that I saw in the making was inspired by Dickens's *A Christmas Carol*. It imagined a grown-up Timothy Cratchit living with a now-kinder Scrooge, but because he yearns for independence, going off on his own for a series of adventures in London.

Thomas Cote, the director of the production and the artistic director of the theater, invited me to one of the rehearsals. The cast of ten had only started rehearsing together a few days earlier, and as I watched them run through the play, I did not see how they could possibly put on a credible performance just a few nights later.

The group was mainly practicing musical numbers, which confused me, because I hadn't known the play was a musical. The actor playing the character of Grimaldi, a self-important circus clown who refuses to acknowledge he's a has-been, and whose company Timothy has joined on his journey of self-discovery, appeared nervous and often fumbled the lyrics.

Cote, the director, came up to me and explained: "He's freaking out because he's not a singer. But that's okay because he's a great actor and his character doesn't need to be a good singer." The rest of the cast was better at singing, but their delivery of both spoken and musical words was often tentative and uncoordinated.

Michael Roberts, the composer and pianist, was encouraging, as were Cote, and Knee, who was also in attendance. The three of them frequently expressed gratitude to the actors. But I found out later that despite his smiles and praise, Knee had been freaking out inside, and Roberts had been none too confident, either.

It was with a sense of dread that I attended the concert reading of the play a few nights later. At this intermediate stage in the play's life, the actors were not in costume and they simply stood as they read from the bound script in front of them. Still, it was a full run-through in front of an audience.

I was floored by how polished the performance was compared with the jerky, uncertain version I had seen two nights earlier. Something truly magical had occurred in the intervening time. The actor playing Grimaldi was confident and convincing. A soaring and haunting solo sung by one of the actresses, called "Bright White Speckled Lark," stayed in my head all the next day.

A few weeks after the concert reading, I met with Knee, Cote, and Roberts at Roberts's home in Manhattan's Murray Hill to discuss the evolution of the play. It turned out that the play had not even been a musical originally. Knee had enlisted Roberts to add music to a few of the play's scenes, but when the two of them met for several hours, two weeks before the first rehearsal, they decided it could work as a musical.

"I didn't know where we were going when we began," Knee said of that initial meeting. Knee said he had a visceral, instinctive reaction that he could work with Roberts. It was almost as if Roberts could read Knee's mind. And so Knee was receptive to the idea of turning the play into a musical—for which Roberts said he could, and did, write all the songs in the space of two weeks.

Knee confessed that he had been extremely upset the night of the rehearsal I had attended (although he hid it very well). Cote calmed him down later with four or five long texts. Knee questioned why Cote was letting the actors just run through the material without stopping them with suggestions for improvement. "I felt that the actors didn't need me harping in their ear about every moment," Cote explained to me.

Roberts, too, had been anxious during the very rough rehearsal. "I always think about it like war," he told me. "The captain who's leading the soldiers into battle has just as good a chance at getting shot as everybody else. He's as scared as everybody else. The only difference is, he just cannot show it."

The entire next day, Roberts worked individually with the actor playing Grimaldi to prepare him for his singing parts, and that work clearly paid off.

Looking back, Knee said, "It's when I doubted, and Tom brought me back to sanity that was the most exciting time. You think, Oh no, this is not going to work, and then you find a way to make it work."

Cote knew the actors were going to sleep on the material and absorb it, and "what happened Thursday night is that the thing exploded. All ten of them, they just jumped into it."

"The project that the three of us are working on right now is considered much more of a passion project," Cote said. When millions of dollars are sitting on the table it becomes a whole different beast because then it's a business as well as a creative proposition.

Collaboration on this level has to be fun, Cote said. "If it's not fun, it's not worth doing." It doesn't mean you're not having disagreements, "but it's critical that everybody feel like this is fun and joyful."

For Knee, collaboration is a welcome opportunity to escape from the isolation and self-doubt of writing. Collaborators can pull you through by believing in you more than you believe in yourself, he said.

When it's good, collaboration "really enriches me as a writer," Knee said. "When it's bad, it kills me. It becomes a very noncreative situation."

Nine months after my warm and fuzzy interview with Knee, Roberts, and Cote, I attended a different play at the WorkShop Theater and saw an advertisement on the program for the Timothy Cratchit play by Allan Knee, with music and lyrics by . . . Andre Catrini. Wait—what had happened to Michael Roberts?

With some trepidation, I emailed Knee, and then Roberts, to ask them what had happened. I interviewed them separately, and their stories differed in some respects, but this much they agreed on: just a few weeks after I talked to them, the two had an argument in a coffee shop and the collaboration abruptly ended. They also agreed that the conflict was over personalities and not over the quality of the work.

I got the sense that some version of the "who's in charge" problem had reared its head here. Knee told me Roberts said something to him along the lines of: I'm not taking orders from you. Roberts told me he felt the two men needed to be more equitable in how they approached their work, and explained that to Knee. It escalated to the point that Roberts left the coffee shop, never to return. Cote totally accepted the situation, and didn't get upset with either of them, both said. He has maintained a good relationship with both.

Some of their conflicts may have arisen from the fact that Knee and Roberts had different upbringings and express their emotions differently. Knee readily acknowledges that he grew up in a crazy, difficult household, and "I do get emotional when I'm not heard." Roberts was raised in a more stable home and said he doesn't get angry unless it's absolutely necessary. Maybe Knee wanted Roberts to get angry alongside him, and he just wouldn't do that, Roberts mused.

Both men have put the episode behind them and say they have no regrets. Roberts is busy with other productions. He got custody of the songs, and I'm sure we'll be hearing "Bright White Speckled Lark" spotlighted in some other production someday. What he learned from the experience, he said, "is that you don't have to go through a torturous process that isn't working. You can extricate yourself from that."

Knee said: "I was very upset when it ended—I was rattled by it and confused, but I'm not sorry about it anymore. I know I'm working with someone who's more compatible with me."

I saw the play during the 2015 holiday season. It was, of course, different from the version I had witnessed earlier that year. Not only were the songs completely new, but there were several new actors, including a new Grimaldi. But the bones of the play were the same, and much of the original version remained. In a sense, the people who had left were still making a contribution. Knee had loved "Bright White Speckled Lark," too; he said Catrini's initial song for that part of the play had not risen to that level. So Knee pressed him to come up with something better, and he did.

What is one of the main things that can get in the way of collaboration? The experts I talked to tended to give one answer: egos. Sometimes, egos can simply overwhelm a group. In that case, it can be more productive to have the artistic visionary meet with just one other person rather than in a group, Elsbach said. Some artists work so well in a dyad that they come to include the other person in their self-identity, she added.

In his book *Powers of Two*, Joshua Wolf Shenk discusses the importance of the dyad in numerous creative groups, including the Beatles. In some pairs, as with Lennon and McCartney, the two members are equally celebrated. In others, one person "takes the lone-genius spotlight while the other remains in history's shadows." Many husband-and-wife teams have operated this way, with the long-suffering wife tending to get short shrift in the credit department. Vladimir and Véra Nabokov are a famous example of this type of pairing.

Pairs can merge their identities while making up for each other's deficiencies. The star needs a director. The dreamer needs a doer. The anarchist needs an organizer. In the case of the Beatles, McCartney was the charmer, the diplomat, and the organizer while Lennon was the agitator, the iconoclast, and the disrupter. Inevitably, these differences led to tensions and eventually a breakup. Any kind of collaboration, and especially that between a pair, involves a carefully calibrated harnessing of talents and tension.

These complementarities and conflicts played out in one of the most celebrated pairings in Silicon Valley history: that of Steve Jobs and Steve Wozniak of Apple. Jobs was the visionary, while Wozniak was the practical engineer.

Nevertheless, in the history of technological innovation you can see a constant tug-of-war between wanting credit, ownership, and profit on the one hand, and seeking to build and share knowledge on the other.

Some people crave credit—either for their own personal glory or for the financial rewards that accrue from it. The history of technological innovation is filled with examples of scientists who were reluctant or unwilling to share credit for breakthroughs that could never have happened without the insights and contributions of others (in a few cases they even stole the credit).

Credit is a murky issue. "Great innovations are usually the result of ideas that flow from a large number of sources," Walter Isaacson writes in his book *The Innovators*. "An invention, especially one as complex as the computer, usually comes not from an individual brainstorm but from a collaboratively woven tapestry of creativity."

"When people take insights from multiple sources and put them together, it's natural for them to think that the resulting ideas are their own—as in truth they are," he says. "All ideas are born that way." It is ironic that both the Internet and Wikipedia—the ultimate in collaborative inventions—were the source of intense squabbling over who deserved most of the credit for creating them.

The Internet offers an unprecedented opportunity to form creative teams with people from all over the world—people one never need meet in person, and in real time, too. This is an astonishing development that most people could not have imagined fifty years ago. The far-flung people on these teams can perform piece work, as it were, doing the more tedious or time-consuming tasks, thereby freeing up the project leaders for the bigger, idea-driven efforts. Or they can participate full-throttle in the enterprise, thanks to text, chat, Skype, and other technological innovations.

Parag Chordia and Prerna Gupta were able to develop their music apps with the help of two people in Ukraine they found through the freelance website Elance. They never met the two men in person and only talked directly to the project manager once, over Skype. Realizing that he was uncomfortable with voice interaction, they communicated by text ever after. They never spoke directly to the developer, Pavel—"at least I think his name was Pavel; that's what I was told," Gupta said.

But at their heart, the Songify and LaDiDa apps were the result of a collaborative dyad consisting of Gupta and Chordia.

LaDiDa is based on work that Chordia did as a professor at Georgia Tech along with his graduate students, related to an artificial intelligence technology called reverse karaoke. The technology can "listen" to what a person is singing and compose music to go along with it. When the iPhone came out in 2007, Gupta realized that Chordia's research project had serious consumer potential. Gupta could never have created the app without the technical know-how of Chordia and his developers, and they could never have designed a popular iPhone app without Gupta's consumer-facing focus.

With LaDiDa and later apps, "I was more or less in charge of figuring out from a user's perspective what the product would be," Gupta said. She was crucial to the apps' success because she wasn't so immersed in the technical details and didn't exactly know what was technically feasible. On several occasions, she pushed the engineers to pull off something that they had originally not thought possible—such as breaking speech into smaller increments so that it sounded like rap. (A key insight was that all the syllables in rap are roughly the same length in time, as opposed to everyday speech, where they are all over the place.)

It was a matter of riffing on ideas, experimenting with how different things sounded, and finding out through trial and error if their experiments could exist, technically, in an app. Once the developers found the technical solutions, they then needed Gupta's help to simplify the way they were presented so that users could grasp them easily.

For Gupta, the hardest part of developing the apps was translating the vision she had in her head into something that could actually work. She felt that collaboration made that easier. It's easy to convince yourself that something will resonate with the outside world because it resonates with you, but that is often not the case, she said. Collaborators offer more of a reality test.

Chordia and Gupta created a company called Khush to sell their apps. Khush soon caught the eye of a similar company called Smule, which acquired it, bringing Chordia and Gupta a tidy sum. After staying at Smule for a short while, Gupta left the company along with Chordia to take some time off, mainly in Costa Rica. When I talked to them, they were working on their next big project.

Chordia said he and Gupta are good at "thinking about what's at the edge of possibility." That's where their next project comes in—they're creating a fiction app for young adults, with the story unfolding via text messages written by the characters. As Gupta put it, it's storytelling for the Snapchat generation.

The form bears some resemblance to a traditional epistolary novel, except that it demands much more brevity and constraint from the author. "It forces a certain discipline. It forces you to plot out the entire thing beforehand and make sure all the pieces fit," Chordia said.

"When you're messaging someone, you're not giving them the version you would give them if you were speaking to them," he said. "You're giving them a more concise version, a punchier version." He and Gupta are experimenting with the boundaries of the medium, and they are enlisting readers as collaborators.

Through ads on Facebook, they find people to click on the app for free, and then they track their readers' progress. Say a story has 100 messages, for a total of about 1,000 words. They can draw a graph that shows how many people started, how many got to the end, and where and how many dropped off in the middle. On some of their test stories, they have seen a completion rate of 80 percent.

They are proceeding incrementally, and have slowly added free-lance writers as collaborators to test out more stories. They hope to add stories later with a longer narrative arc. They have formed a company called Hooked to market the app and other products that spring from it. Readers will be able to create their own stories on the app too, Gupta said. "We think it's a very natural platform for our demographic to tell stories," Chordia added. If all goes as planned, they would like to self-publish a full-length book after the app and from there produce a movie or a television show based on the story.

Old-fashioned reader that I am, I bristle at the idea of someone monitoring my reading behavior. Chordia stressed that the analysis would be anonymous, but I was still bothered by the privacy implications, even though data analysis like this is starting to be embedded in the fabric of modern life.

Also, if audience metrics are used to determine the quality of an artistic product, and the original creator revises the product based on those metrics, then the artist's singular vision could be lost in favor of pandering to the reader with empty, melodramatic plot twists.

Gupta and Chordia are fully aware of this danger. In the end, they assert, their artistic vision will have the final say.

Raised as I was on the myth of the romantic genius, I was unsettled to hear the act of artistic creation broken down into pieces and discussed as if it were a mere product, manufactured in a kind of fiction factory.

And yet in the 1930s, the making of films was explicitly modeled after the Ford automotive assembly line. Literary giants including William Faulkner, F. Scott Fitzgerald, and Nathanael West agreed to become factory workers of a sort, writing screenplays for the studios when the fruits of their individual efforts failed to pay the bills.

In Hollywood, filmmaking began as a highly collaborative and also a corporate art form, said Jeremy Braddock, an associate professor at Cornell University who is interested in examples of collective authorship.

There is a tendency in our culture to see artists as autonomous geniuses, but film is an especially problematic art form in which to hold this view, Braddock said. In fact, the notion that the director is the author of a film was introduced very late in the history of the form.

The idea of the directorial "auteur" began to emerge in the late 1960s and early '70s with directors like Martin Scorsese and Francis Ford Coppola. The studios, in a period of financial distress, were willing to give these directors far more individual control than ever before, with the result that they were culturally recognized as authors and even marketed by the studios as such. You would never have seen "A Martin Scorsese Film" in 1950, Braddock said.

The result was that directors now had reputations to guard. Directors began to object that the final versions of their films were not what they had intended, and they applied to the Directors Guild of

America to have a pseudonym used in the credits. As more directors began requesting pseudonyms, the Directors Guild of America decreed that disputed films could carry only one fake director's name: Allen (or Alan) Smithee.

An Alan Smithee in the credits often signals creative differences with the studio or a lead actor. Maybe the director fought with an actor and quit in a huff, and then the new director who stepped in to replace the aggrieved one felt strange about taking the credit. Other times, a director disagreed with the final cut—it was too long, or more likely too short, or emphasized the wrong scenes.

For the most part, directors simply cannot carry off the role of "auteur," Ed Catmull, president of Pixar Animation and Disney Animation, said in an interview. What others would term collaboration, the auteur director might consider to be interference. But directors need the feedback of others, Catmull said.

At a certain point, most directors flounder in their own films, he said, and they lose objectivity. That's why he organized the Braintrust, a group of company writers, directors, and heads of story who give a director feedback on a film in progress.

The feedback must be candid because "without the critical ingredient that is candor, there can be no trust," Catmull writes in his book, *Creativity, Inc.* "And without trust, creative collaboration is not possible."

The Braintrust doesn't have actual authority over the director, Catmull told me. That frees up the director to listen, he said, echoing Kimberly Elsbach's findings with the toy designers. Eventually, authority figures do have their input, but not right away.

But that's not enough. Before the final version, Pixar holds an audience screening so the director can see the film through its eyes. It's an in-person version of Chordia and Gupta's testing platform. The audience members have no personal stake in the film. The director can see how well his or her ideas are being communicated by how rapt and responsive the audience is. Just the act of sitting in the audience makes the director more objective, Catmull said.

Catmull has built these forms of feedback into the structure of Pixar because he knows that showing your work to others is a kind of personal exposure that can be painful. When the directors go through that, "you have to give them some support," he said.

When he started to write *Creativity, Inc.*, Catmull assumed that he would eventually go through a mini-version of what his directors always experienced: getting lost for a time and then needing feedback to find the right path.

So first off he got a cowriter: Amy Wallace, who he knew would provide a different viewpoint. They went through two versions, at which point Catmull knew he needed more feedback. "So I did the equivalent of an audience screening. I asked forty people to read the book." A third of the readers were within Pixar or Disney. Another third knew the history of the company. The other third were writers who were not as familiar with the company or its history.

After he received all the comments, he assembled them into a single document and from the whole discovered a series of problems with the book that no one person would have named. It was especially helpful that some directors and writers in the group identified a structural problem that was much easier for them to see than most people, because that is the way they think when they work on films.

Catmull thinks that the idea of an individual creative genius is an illusion. "In fact, almost everything great is the result of a collaboration between people," he said. Even with seemingly solo endeavors, it's important to accept that "the people who precede you and the people around you are all sources of inspiration and influence on what you do."

TEN

Love and Work

*L*ove *and work are central* to our humanness, Freud is reported to have said. It is in these two realms that we yearn most deeply for fulfillment.

We borrow from the language of love when we talk about work, and vice versa. We say we feel passion for a creative project—or that it is "our baby." And to love another person, we say, requires hard work and struggle. The crossing over of the terms reflects the supreme importance of these two psychic tentpoles in our lives.

A lasting relationship has a long arc and a structure; so does a big creative project. As the psychoanalyst Ethel Person wrote, "Love is an act of imagination. For some of us, it will be the great creative triumph of our lives." Love, Person said, "allows us both to renew and transform ourselves." So does work. Both love and work, at their highest levels, achieve a seeming paradox. They make us deeply aware of our inner self, and they also allow us to transcend that self. Both lead to higher states of consciousness and cause us to grow as humans.

That was true for Jack Roberts, a friend of mine who is one of the people I asked, while writing this book: "What's your Big Thing?" For him, the biggest creative project of his life was the relationship he had with his partner, Rick Schaub.

"One of the things that brought us together and held us together was that we both really loved working on houses," Roberts said. "We had six different houses in fourteen years." They would fix up one house, sell it, and move to a somewhat more expensive fixer-upper with the money they had made from their previous house—all as housing prices kept rising in Portland, Oregon, where they lived.

These were houses in up-and-coming neighborhoods with a lot of potential. "We learned a lot," Roberts said. "We added bathrooms, we remodeled kitchens." Now he can do the electrical wiring for a house on his own.

"We both had full-time jobs," Roberts said. "We would come home from work and we would do Sheetrock or wiring until eleven at night and fall into bed and then get up at six in the morning and go to work. We loved it. It really was creative." They sold two of the houses to friends of theirs, who continue to live in those houses.

"For us, having houses and working on houses and our interest in houses really did provide substance to our relationship," Roberts said.

Rick died of AIDS in the mid-1990s, when the two were both in their early forties. "That was the big project of my life—being with him," Roberts said. "I think if he hadn't died, we would have stayed together. It seemed like we had a pretty good way of working out our problems." Now, he said, "I have this wonderful foundation for my life of having been in love with someone in a successful way."

Living together as a gay couple in the 1980s and '90s was not easy, and finding a way to make that work took creativity in itself. They were living in a historical fault line between secrecy and openness. Bridging that gap together was exciting and challenging.

"I'll never forget the first time we wanted to buy a house together," Roberts said. "We just looked at each other—can two men get a mortgage together?" Part of the reason they worked on the houses themselves was that they were afraid that electricians and plumbers might be intolerant of their lifestyle. Usually they were the only gay couple in their neighborhood. And Rick was a public schoolteacher who had to pretend he was straight to all but his closest friends and colleagues. "It was a real project to create a way to be a gay couple," Roberts said.

Our current online era works against achieving love with this kind of long arc, just as it hinders long-term creative projects, by offering myriad little magnets for our attention. We become so distracted that it's hard to concentrate on just one person or one project.

Online dating offers so many choices that it can be hard to commit to just one. I've seen friends on dating apps and sites swipe left or click to the next option in less than a second, rejecting a potential date based on a fleeting view of a photo. I'd been guilty of these split-second appraisals, too, although mainly I'd dropped out of the dating game altogether.

But then, as I was working on this chapter, it occurred to me: just as I'd been procrastinating on writing a book, I'd also been procrastinating in my love life.

For decades, because I had built up an idealized mental image of what my book would be, I was unable to work on it. Only by securing an outside deadline for it and doing the imperfect and incremental work of writing it was I finally able to make it happen.

Similarly, after building up an idealized image of the perfect man (ever since reading *Jane Eyre* at age ten), I have often failed to take the steps needed to form a lasting, if imperfect, relationship. My depression had a lot to do with that; it distorted my view of myself as a potential romantic partner. A few times I've been able to break through that. I had one major relationship in my twenties, another in my thirties, and some flings in my forties and fifties.

For the sake of this book, I reasoned, I needed to give romance another try. My dating foray came as I sought to answer some big questions: Are there similarities between the urge to find love and the artistic urge to create? Does finding and sustaining love require hard work in the same way that a creative endeavor does? Can artistic expression be a substitute for romantic love if you don't have a partner?

In the midst of all this I went to see Paulette Sherman, a psychologist who specializes as a dating coach. She has also written several books about dating, and was happy to help me find parallels between dating and writing a book—and maybe even leverage the book as a way to find love.

When I visited her Manhattan office, Sherman asked me about my process for writing this book. I explained that although my methods were flawed, I had managed to develop a monthly routine that roughly started with two weeks of research and ended with two weeks of writing. Sherman quickly grasped that I liked structure, needed a deadline, and had to be accountable to someone before I could move forward.

Then she asked me: "What process do you have right now for your dating?" My response was to laugh.

"You're laughing," she said, "but you're expecting results without a process."

Sherman has written about using your work ethic to find love. Despite starry-eyed notions to the contrary, many people need to put serious effort into finding a partner, she said. (They tend to get annoyed when she tells them this.)

The first part of the effort is internal, she said: removing any mental obstacles that prevent you from finding a partner. Too many people cling to limiting beliefs from the past rather than focusing on the present reality. "We limit ourselves before we even start, and how we perceive ourselves is often translated into how others perceive us," she said.

She advised me to make a list of my limiting beliefs and then challenge them. One of mine, held over from junior high, is that I am not attractive (if you'll recall, I recently had a dream where I was afraid the police were going to arrest me for trying to be sexy), when in point of fact some men (not a flood of them, it's true, but a few) have shown clear signs of being attracted to me.

Sherman also suggested something truly cheesy: to make a list of twenty-five qualities that make me a great catch, and look at them right before a date. That was going too far. I did make the list, but I was too embarrassed to look at it more than once.

The second part of Sherman's plan was action-oriented: taking practical steps to meet people face-to-face. She became the equivalent of a teacher who gave me an assignment and a deadline. And because I wanted to be a good student I got my assignment done.

The assignment was to set up a profile on Match.com, which I had been thinking about doing for the last three years. But because I was now accountable to someone else, my dating coach, I finally took the incremental steps—finding some photos, taking a few selfies, writing a profile, answering the questions on the site—to make it happen.

After I set up the profile, Sherman said, it would be a good idea to spend ten minutes each day—with an egg timer by my side, if necessary—to send out emails to potential dates. You can't just wait for men to write to you, she stressed. Ideally she likes people to be on three dating sites at once and arrange two dates a week.

This seemed so calculating, and I also knew what would happen: most of the men wouldn't be interested. I date so seldom that any rejection really hurts. I recounted to Sherman how I had met someone for a date two months earlier and—the old story—he'd said he would definitely call. He even emailed me a few times afterward, but then I never heard from him again. "It takes me about six weeks to get over something like that," I told her forlornly.

"Because you're not used to it," she said. "When you date all the time that's pretty common." If you can look at it as a process that takes time, it's not as taxing emotionally, she said. Similarly, if you're an author, even if many, many publishers reject you, you only need one, she said. You need to have that sort of resolve.

Of course there were no guarantees that I would find someone, but I asked her: "Do you think there's a chance?" (Maybe this wasn't just for the book, after all.)

"I do. I always think there's a chance. And I definitely think that about you because you seem like a lovely person." Just think of dates as experiences in the present moment and don't get ahead of yourself, she advised.

*   *   *

This sounded very familiar—it was similar to what my posture teacher, Lindsay Newitter, had told me about writing a book.

Earlier, Lindsay had come to my home and helped me adjust my furniture and physical stance so I could work on my book more comfortably. She had warned me against moving my mind—and my body along with it—into the future without fully occupying the present. Given that this is a serious danger not just with writing but also with dating, I wondered: Could Lindsay help me with my dating posture?

After my first session with Sherman, I sent Lindsay an email: "I am going to try online dating (ugh!), and it occurred to me that it would help to have a dating posture lesson. They do say it's about how you 'carry yourself.' It also occurred to me that often when we date we are guilty of 'endgaining,' in that we look ahead to marriage, etc., rather than experiencing the present moment with the person across the table from us."

Lindsay thought that this would be an interesting avenue to explore, and it was high time I had a posture tune-up anyway, so I met with her for two more lessons. Lindsay said I was on the right track making parallels between my book and dating. How you exist in your physical space affects both your creativity and the way you interact with another person. In both cases, achieving the best stance can be a pathway to openness—to ideas and people. It comes down to this: How is the way you are using your body affecting the things that are important to you?

At my lesson I began by saying that I'm never really sure how I'm supposed to sit on a date, because I don't want to lean into a man with my cleavage but neither do I want to seem too stiff and formal.

"You can be casual and not have horrible posture," Lindsay assured me. She demonstrated by slouching backward in a loose-limbed manner in her chair. "I'm sitting badly in a way," she said. "But nonetheless I'm maintaining my internal expansiveness. I still have contact with the chair, and my feet are on the floor. I'm thinking about all those points expanding away from each other. So I'm not pressing myself together even though I'm not in a perfectly aligned state."

When you maintain your internal expansiveness, you come across as more calm, centered, and confident, she said, and more present. Your composure (or lack of it) can influence the person you're interacting with.

As an example of what not to do, she sat on the edge of her seat, tightened her neck, and pulled her shoulders in. "It's like I'm getting a little ahead of myself."

"You're endgaining," I said. "'Is this my future husband?'"

"So I might come on a little strong or I might not really be taking the person in."

On the other hand, you can also relax to such an extreme that you become disengaged—as if you don't have any interest in the person across from you, she said.

What she was telling me was similar to what the dating coach had said, and in more general terms what my mindfulness teacher had discussed. Whether I'm working on a book or dating, I may bring certain negative habits and beliefs from my past into the present. And I may also project myself so far ahead into an imagined future that I lose sight of my experience in the present.

For the headline of my Match.com profile I wrote: "Love and Work: Are There Similarities?" In my profile, in addition to describing myself, I wrote: "I'm currently writing a book about creativity and would be interested to hear your thoughts on parallels between doing creative work and finding love."

Gratifyingly, I did receive some winks, likes, and emails, but only one person responded to my query about love and work. It's mainly about the photos, I guess.

"Not sure if there are too many parallels—they're almost opposites," responded M., sixty-five and divorced, of Brooklyn. "Creative work requires concentration, introspection and a lot of practice—often makes it difficult to fit someone else into your life. There's a reason why highly creative people—great artists, musicians, writers, etc.—so often have troubled personal lives. They become 'married' to their art."

Good answer! And he didn't look too bad, so I emailed him and we arranged to meet for dinner at a Turkish restaurant in Manhattan.

He was certainly one of the oddest people I have ever been on a date with. He reminded me of Jack Nicholson, and of Jack Benny, with wild, sparse hair and contorted mannerisms. He immediately began grilling me on my book and continued to question the premise of this chapter. He wasn't being mean, from what I could tell—just calling it as he saw it in his hyperanalytical way.

I wasn't surprised that he worked as a software programmer. I felt as if almost everything I said was being taken apart, reassembled, and submitted to me for a meaningful response that I was dutybound to provide. I was too busy keeping up with him to think about my posture much at all.

But at the end of my two hours with M., I did notice that my body and mind were exhausted, and it was probably for the best that we did not end up meeting again.

In the following few weeks, I tried to put serious effort into online dating, and I did meet a few other interesting men, although nothing came of those dates, either. Maybe, I thought, if I kept on making the effort, week after week after week, I could find someone with whom to build a long-term relationship.

I have met men and women who went on dates with more than two hundred people before they found someone to settle down with. They made finding love a priority and put the work—sometimes tedious, sometimes frustrating—into achieving it.

Some people are magically able to skip that step. Love does fall out of the sky for some, just as the songs describe. That was the case for a nineteen-year-old art student named Noriko, who arrived in New York from Japan in the early 1970s. By accident she wandered into a Soho art studio and met Ushio Shinohara, a forty-one-year-old who was a brash presence on the avant-garde art scene. He was known for his sculptures of motorcycles and his "action" paintings, where he applied paint to boxing gloves and attacked large canvases with them in a two-minute right-to-left artistic assault.

Noriko was swept up by Ushio's passion and creativity, and they soon married and had a child. His work, while acknowledged by critics as significant, proved hard to sell, resulting in continual financial hardship. As Noriko assisted Ushio with his art and cared for their son, Alex, she had little time to pursue her own artistic ambitions. Ushio was also an alcoholic. Their meeting may have been effortless, but their marriage—at least for Noriko—proved to be hard work.

People often say that keeping a marriage strong requires sustained effort. There are romantic and fun and fulfilling parts, but also tedious and annoying and painful parts. It always falls short of the ideal, and requires a deep commitment to get past the most difficult phases of it. This is true of a Big Thing, too.

Several decades into the Shinoharas' marriage, the balance shifted, and Noriko came into her own. Their relationship, by turns contentious and affectionate, is described in the Oscar-nominated 2013 documentary *Cutie and the Boxer,* by Zachary Heinzerling.

At the beginning of the movie, we see Noriko assisting Ushio with one of his massive canvases in progress. Ushio, still vigorous and ambitious at eighty, says of his wife: "She is just an assistant. The average one has to support the genius." As with many of his comments, it's hard to tell whether he is joking or serious—probably a bit of both. He and Noriko clearly enjoy ribbing each other, and contradicting the other's statements.

"I'm not his assistant." Noriko asserts. "But sometimes I help because it's an emergency."

In the twenty-first century, Ushio is still having trouble selling his work, and he and Noriko are forever struggling to make ends meet. "I should've married a guy who made a secure living and took responsibility for what he did," Noriko laments in the movie.

"I did the best I could to raise my child," she says. "Because he came from a poor family with an alcoholic parent, he had a strong inferiority complex. I feel guilty that I didn't give my son a proper environment to grow up in, with a drunk adult hanging around all the time." By the time of the movie, health problems have forced Ushio to quit drinking, and their life is more stable. Meanwhile, Alex, born and raised amid a morass of art supplies, has become a struggling artist just like his parents.

At first, Ushio was Noriko's teacher, and she felt inferior to him, but slowly that changed. In the movie, a gallery owner comes to see Ushio's work at his studio in Brooklyn, and Noriko asks him to take a look at her own work: a series of drawings, called *Cutie and the Boxer*, that are based on her conflicted relationship with Ushio (called Bullie in the drawings).

After seeing her work, the gallery owner wants to show both Ushio's and Noriko's work in one show, much to Ushio's amazement. (The catalog, Ushio complains to a friend, "starts off talking about important artist couples. What the hell? That's crazy!") The movie shows Noriko recreating the story of Cutie and Bullie on a large canvas in the gallery.

"Cutie had a life of struggle," Noriko says of her creation. "But after a while she becomes more independent. Now, Cutie defeats Bullie. She conquers him. She controls him. Cutie is very good at taming Bullie. But it's not so easy to tame him in real life."

Noriko has achieved a measure of independence in real life, even if Ushio still tries to dominate her. At one point, in one of the couple's typical mocking exchanges, she notes that she is his free secretary, free assistant, and free chef. "If you are rich, you can kick me out. You are poor. That's why you are with me."

"I need you," Ushio says emphatically, patting her fondly, and then adds, "Cutie hates Bullie."

"No," says Noriko. "Cutie loves Bullie so much."

"My life with Ushio has been a constant struggle," she says in a voice-over. "But that has made me who I am today. Now I think all of that struggle was necessary for my art. And if I had to do it over again, I would."

I wanted to see how the Shinoharas were doing two years after the movie came out, so I visited their ramshackle combined home and studio in the Dumbo (from "down under the Manhattan Bridge overpass") neighborhood of Brooklyn.

I was met by their son, Alex, who was living and working in the apartment, too. Since the film, Ushio had moved his studio from across the street to a space above his apartment, and he was working when I came to see him, the room chaotic with brushes and paints and dozens of sculptures and huge rolled-up canvases.

At eighty-three, Ushio remained muscular and energetic, and he filled the room with his good-humored vitality. He wore one of his signature boxing gloves, dipped in blue paint, while we talked. He showed me one of his recent motion paintings, which had taken him two and a half minutes to paint; he hoped to sell it for fifty thousand dollars. Our conversation was a bit halting because his English is not quite fluent—in the film, his dialogue is mostly Japanese, translated into English subtitles.

I asked him: "Do you see any similarity between making art and a marriage?"

"Marriage is completely different because marriage is convenient," he said with a laugh. "My wife and me help each other survive." He said his life is like "living on a bed of nails" because he has no fixed income.

I reminded Ushio that in the movie, when their husband-and-wife show is about to open, Noriko asks him if he's jealous, and he says, "Yes, jealous!"

That was just pretend, he told me now. In the art world, he said, he is ten times more important than Noriko, although he acknowledged that his wife's future is bright.

Alex works in his father's studio, and he showed me some of his drawings and sculptures. I was struck by how some of the sculptures seemed to be an amalgam of his parents' work. They resembled the bulbous human figures of Noriko's *Cutie and the Boxer* drawings along with the color and bulk of Ushio's motorcycle sculptures. Within the family I was getting a sense of artistic influence extending three ways—along with a strong sense of individuality and competition.

No matter how hard I tried, I could not get Ushio and Noriko to sit together and talk. So Alex, their joint creation, took me down a floor to talk separately with Noriko, who was sitting at a workstation in a corner. She seemed so busy and intent that I didn't want to bother her, but Alex said it would be okay. Noriko arose and sat across from me at a long table, her gray hair styled in her trademark braided pigtails.

When I told Noriko that her husband had said he was not actually jealous of her, she said, "All artists are jealous. And men are more jealous than women."

"So he really is jealous of you," I said.

"Of course."

In the documentary, Noriko alludes to Virginia Woolf's view that in order to create fiction, and by extension all art, "a woman must have money and a room of her own."

When the movie was being made, Noriko and Ushio often worked in the large room that we were now sitting in because Ushio did not want to walk across the street to his studio. Ushio was constantly interrupting her, she said, so she made a rule: when she was working in her space in the corner, it was to be considered an independent country and nobody could enter it without a visa. She would allow visitors to have a visa, but not him. Still, he interrupted her.

Things are better now that Ushio has his own space one floor above, she said—now he can go there easily, even in the middle of the night. But her dream is "to have a studio far away so he cannot interrupt at all. But I need more money."

As a result of the movie, Noriko said, more people recognize Ushio and her on the street and in cafes, and it's made them proud. "But survival with art is still so difficult."

There is no doubt that Ushio has stimulated Noriko artistically, but as she says in the movie, "We are like two flowers in one pot. Sometimes we don't get enough nutrients for both of us. But when everything goes well we become two beautiful flowers. So it's either heaven or hell."

In her book Grown-Up Marriage, Judith Viorst writes: "In a grown-up marriage we gradually acquire a rueful tolerance of each other's limitations and imperfections." Marriage demands "vast stores of patience. It requires paying attention, more attention than we've ever paid before. It requires compelling ourselves, when we are sick and tired and ready to slam the door, to nonetheless leave the door just slightly ajar.

"Marriage teaches all of us that we won't get all we expected— some of the time, most of the time, or ever. It teaches us that, unless we're incredibly lucky, we're going to have to work hard for what we want.

"So now the work begins, the work of: Accepting the flawed, imperfect person we've married. Reconciling some—not all, but hopefully enough—of our difficult differences. Coming to terms with what we can't get, and never are going to get, from each other. Creating, we two together, our 'third thing.'"

This messy work that Viorst describes reminds me in many ways of what I've gone through while writing this book. I've traded my idealized version of a book for the real thing. Will I ever end up doing so with a romantic partner?

I thought I would have to wait until I finished this book to make the effort, because finding and going out on dates was draining me of the willpower I needed to get my writing done, even though I was dating as research for the book—or so I told myself. (It was so confusing.)

But then I started chatting with someone online, and that led to a first date, which I enjoyed, which led me to wonder over and over, Will he call? And as I began to obsess about whether he would call, I forced myself to think about the book instead, and was grateful to have it as a meaningful mental counterweight.

Reader, for the record, he did call, and the second date led to a third and a fourth and more. But as I venture back into the dating scene, the question arises: Is that something I even want? I certainly don't need a romantic partner in my life. Fortunately I have the financial independence to be able to live on my own. And I do have love in my life—the love of friends, family, and pets. I actually have what Noriko Shinohara says she has always wanted: money and a room of my own. On the other hand, I'm sure I've been lonely in ways that she never has.

At my age, and given my peculiarities, I can't help thinking that my chances of finding long-term love are slim. So at some point should I just give up? In Chapter 6, I urged people to consider giving up on creative projects that they have carried around in their heads for years without working on them. What a relief it would be if I could do that with my dream of finding a partner—if I could say with finality, "This is not going to happen. You can be happy with the life you have." But I can't quite do that. I can even imagine myself in my nineties in the ICU, on the brink of death, thinking, Is that man in the bed over there single?

How many people experience complete happiness in love and work, at the same time or ever? What makes us fully human, in the Freudian sense, is not necessarily achieving, but striving toward happiness in these two areas, ruing their lack and making up for them in other ways.

Some people who have a stable romantic partner find it easier to complete their Big Things, as they nestle in the other's warmth and support. In the case of Prerna Gupta and Parag Chordia, whom I wrote about in my chapter on collaboration, that includes working together on the same artistic project. For couples like Noriko and Ushio Shinohara, the relationship is more conflicted, with the partners helping each other, but also obstructing and annoying each other. Or, as M. from Match.com said, being committed to a creative project can make it difficult to fit someone into your life at all.

Or, people who feel a dearth of love may try to compensate for it by turning attention to their jobs or to big creative projects. It's a way of filling the emptiness, and it can produce great things. To couples, especially those with children, all that time can look like a luxury.

Children are seriously disruptive at the time you are raising them. "There's the parenting life of our fantasies, and there's the parenting life of our banal, on-the-ground realities," says Jennifer Senior in her book, *All Joy and No Fun*. She notes that children are often antithetical to flow, the absorbed and focused state that the psychologist Mihaly Csikszentmihalyi identifies as a companion of creativity.

Flow does not thrive on distractions. It is "hard enough to achieve if your sole task is trying to care for your kids. But it's even harder if you're trying to care for your children and work at the same time," Senior writes.

But take the long view and children can be as rewarding a creative project as it is possible to imagine. "Children strain our everyday lives," Senior writes, "but also deepen them." They "give us structure, purpose and stronger bonds to the world around us." Choosing parenthood "gives strength and structural integrity to one's life through meaningful tension." And through our nurturing of them with the knowledge that they will outlive us, they offer us a chance for redemption.

When David Brooks, the *New York Times* columnist, asked readers whether they had a purpose in life, many people said they had found their purpose through raising children. He quoted one father who said, "As is often the case, my purpose became clearly evident after I had stopped looking for it. On October 11, 1995, my daughter was born. Beginning with that moment, there has never been the slightest doubt regarding the purpose and source of meaning in my life. Being a father is the most meaningful and rewarding pursuit a man could ever hope to experience."

Some parents are able to complete Big Things despite the challenges involved. Having a full-time job while writing a book is hard enough for me. I would be felled by the additional responsibility of a child. But for people with more energy than I have, even the tiniest windows of the day offer creative opportunities.

In an interview in the *Paris Review*, Toni Morrison recounted how as a single mother with a full-time job, she was forced to get up before dawn to write: "I needed to use the time before they said, Mama—and that was always around five in the morning. Many years later, after I stopped working at Random House, I just stayed at home for a couple of years. I discovered things about myself I had never thought about before. At first I didn't know when I wanted to eat, because I had always eaten when it was lunchtime or dinnertime or breakfast time. Work and the children had driven all of my habits. . . . I didn't know the weekday sounds of my own house; it all made me feel a little giddy.

"I was involved in writing *Beloved* at that time—this was in 1983—and eventually I realized that I was clearer-headed, more confident and generally more intelligent in the morning. The habit of getting up early, which I had formed when the children were young, now became my choice."

The choice of whether to have children in the first place has been a fraught one for Prerna Gupta, who became virtually inseparable from Parag Chordia after they met at an Indian music event in San Francisco in the mid-2000s. He was an academic special-izing in computer music, and she was working, unhappily, at a venture capital firm. Before they met, they were headed in different directions, both geographically and professionally, but falling in love changed all that. They decided to start an Indian social media site together, and after that faltered, they found success through the musical app LaDiDa and a company that sprang from that. Now they are collaborating on an ambitious storytelling app. They started their ventures because they wanted to find a way to both live and work together.

Most couples seem to prefer to go off to different jobs, I noted: they want to get away from each for a little while. But Gupta and Chordia say it feels more natural for them to merge their work and their personal lives. In fact, Gupta said, it was being separated from Chordia at the venture capital job that partly made her feel so dissat-isfied with it.

"But don't you get sick of each other?" I said.

"No," Gupta said with a laugh. "It's one of the things that makes us really unusual." All the successful married cofounders they know say they just like to spend time together, she said.

It used to be that venture capital companies would not invest in a team of married cofounders, for fear that if the relationship broke up the company would, too, Chordia said. But that is starting to change as tech companies like Goodreads, Eventbrite, and SlideShare—all started by married couples—show that it can be done.

If you start out from a position where you are fundamentally happy, and your marriage is a bedrock, then you're in a better po-sition to take risks, Chordia maintained. Being a couple has helped them withstand the roller-coaster ride of startup life, Gupta said: "There are so many emotional ups and downs when you're building something from scratch."

"But don't you feel both those things at the same time?"

"Usually what happens is that we regulate each other," Chordia said, so that if one person is depressed, the other one makes sure to serve as an emotional buoy.

"And of course you both have an intimate understanding of what you're working on," I said. "It's intimate on both levels."

When you're involved in a startup, it can be hard to be married to someone with a "normal" job, Gupta said, based on what she has heard from couples in that situation. Not only does the other spouse lack a complete understanding of what you do, but there's a tendency to want to pretend that things are going well when they aren't, for fear of being judged for embarking on this crazy endeavor.

As married cofounders, Gupta said, "We both understand what's happening. We understand when things are up and down. And we don't have to pretend to each other." And if you aren't married to your cofounder, you may wonder if that person is questioning whether to continue, or thinking of getting another job.

"That could happen with a spouse, too," I pointed out. "Maybe that person's thinking of getting another spouse!"

It helps that both she and Chordia come from a traditional Indian background where you grow up thinking that divorce is not an option, Gupta said.

All this sounded a little sickeningly perfect, and they at least had the grace to acknowledge that. The cynical and mocking Shinoharas were much more entertaining. With Chordia and Gupta, there appeared to be little of the struggle and hardship that experts claim is part and parcel of marriage. Granted, they were still early in their union, and it may well be tested ten, twenty, or thirty years down the line, although I was too polite, and they were too much in love, for me to bring that up.

Unlike the Shinoharas, Gupta and Chordia don't fight very much. "We debate," Gupta said. "But it's always even-keeled. It tends to be a rational debate. If the emotions are starting to escalate we both make an effort to de-escalate." One thing that prevents conflicts—and this is true for team dynamics in general—is that they each have areas of expertise where they have agreed to defer to the other in case of a disagreement.

I asked them: "Do you think that being in love helps your creativity?" Absolutely, they said.

When you're cocreating, you have two different perspectives existing in the same mental space, Chordia said. Many creative pairs develop a kind of love for each other whether they are romantically involved or not, he said. "What does it mean to love someone? It's to have a deep empathetic connection with someone. So I think it's kind of inseparable, love and creativity."

But when you are in love with someone romantically, "you are by the nature of your relationship existing in the same mental space most of the time, so it's easier to click into that when you're creating something together."

Love makes you childlike, he added, which also fosters creativity. Just listen to the cutesy-speak of happily married couples—it's pretty nauseating, but it keeps them childlike and open to new ideas, he said.

And what about actual children? Gupta, thirty-three, had been stressing out about the issue, she said, but had decided that it would be okay to wait at least several years before making a decision. She understands that the love parents have for their children is profound, but feels strongly that the love she has for her husband is also profound—and that it may be preferable to sacrifice parenthood in exchange for experiencing that love.

Maybe you'll leave beautiful artistic creations behind rather than children, I suggested.

Yes, Gupta said. In a way the things that she and Chordia create together are like their babies, although "I don't mean that as a way of diminishing the importance or divinity of a child."

Chordia said that he is very satisfied with the meaning in his life, and one of the reasons is that "I'm birthing things into the world. Part of having a child is that you've brought something unique into the world. Part of doing something genuinely creative is again bringing something unique into the world that will bring a bit of joy. And so in that sense I see it as very parallel."

The time for me to have a child (at least biologically) has come and gone. I never had a burning desire for a baby the way so many women do. But I still want to leave something behind. I want to have contributed to the world somehow—to leave a legacy.

I do feel guilty that I didn't give my mother and father grandchildren. They would have made such excellent and loving grandparents. (My mother has shelves full of toys for the children of friends and neighbors to play with when they visit.) My siblings haven't stepped up to the plate, either, so it looks like the line will end with us— unless my brother makes a midlife move.

Recently, when I was visiting my parents, my father, who is in his mideighties, asked, "So when's the book going to be published?" When I told him, he said, "Well, I guess I'll still be around then." Better if it had been a grandchild, but I guess a book will have to do.

It must be enormously comforting to be lying on one's deathbed and know that one has had children who have had children who may pass your DNA along indefinitely, keeping you alive in a way. Many people want to leave some part of themselves behind after they die. Through genetics is the most primal way. But for those with or without biological children, the nurturing and mentoring of others, along with behavior by example, can be a way to leave a legacy.

People may also seek to leave a legacy through their creative ideas, as expressed in a Big Thing. Some of that may be narcissistic—just as wanting to have children can be narcissistic—but some of it is tied to what the psychoanalyst Erik Erikson referred to as generativity, the desire to give back without needing anything in return. As the author Daniel Goleman told me in an article I wrote for the *Times* on wisdom, this type of giving back could be creative, social, personal, or financial, and "the wisest people do that in a way that doesn't see their lifetime as limiting when this might happen."

Generativity is a self-transcending love. Whatever form it takes, it builds on the strengths one has accrued in childhood and throughout adulthood, until in full maturity it expresses itself in ways that future generations can receive and interpret in ways uniquely their own.

ELEVEN

It All Adds Up

As I prepared to write this final chapter, I put all the previous chapters, the ones I had written month by month, into one file. There were more than 73,000 words. I printed them out double spaced and was astonished at the thickness of the pile. There were 260 pages. It was a lesson to me to trust in the power of increments, no matter how erratically they may accrue.

When I was in my thirties, my therapist pointed out that I had a tendency to discount my accomplishments. That has not changed. Before I put all my words into one file, I felt that I had not worked hard enough on this book. So often, it seemed, I had been either working at my day job, or sleeping, or reading, or going out, or lazing about.

And yet there they were, those 73,000 words, and although I knew that many of them would not end up in the published book, I also knew that they were far from nonsense. So clearly I had been working on my Big Thing with some degree of persistence. My inner discounter had been wrong.

How much better a book would this have been if I gotten up every single day from 7 to 9 a.m. to work on it, and again in the evening from 9 to 10?

That had been my fantasy at the start of this project. Instead, on many, many mornings, despite having planned, even vowed, to work on the book, I lolled in my bed, played with my cat, read a Scandinavian mystery, and fell back asleep.

Beautiful wisps of sentences appeared in my head as I lay in bed. I must write them down, I thought, but not yet. It felt so good to lie down, basking in the potential of my words.

And then, once I got up, there were things I needed to check: my email, my Facebook, my Twitter account, the papers, Match.com. After I had done all these things, it would be time to go to work, or, if it was the weekend, to go back to bed and read.

I berated myself for procrastinating. I imagined a man barging into my apartment every morning at seven with a gun. Pointing it at my head he would say, "Over to your desk. Now!" Then I would get over to the desk right away. "Now start writing," he would say. Then I would start writing with great urgency.

Or I imagined my very own Céleste, like the one who paved the way for Proust to write *Remembrance of Things Past*. A little before seven she would let herself in and begin to prepare my cafe au lait. Slowly I would awaken to the fragrant smell of the coffee. "Madame Korkki!" she would say brightly, as I had instructed her to do. "You must begin writing soon." There might be a bit of melodramatic resistance on my part, but she would be used to that; it would be our morning joke. She would cajole me into sitting up, hand me my notebook and pen, plump up my pillows, and make sure I began to write, as was her duty.

When I started this book, I thought I would develop a regular daily routine. So many writers and researchers had said this was necessary, and it made sense. People said it was best to get work done in the morning. That is when our brains are freshest and when our dose of willpower is at its peak.

When I began the first chapter I was so proud of myself because I made drinking my first cup of coffee contingent on getting up to write. Well, that lasted for about four weeks. Then my routine began falling apart. According to William James, if I could just keep at the new habit, suffering no exception to occur, then it might begin to take hold. The effort involved in the new behavior, as confirmed by recent research, would gradually become automatic and then be offloaded to my basal ganglia in the form of a habit.

But apparently at my age the doors to my basal ganglia are nearly closed. I was too old to develop a regular daily habit of working on my book. My brain had hardened and could not be cured of its natural indolence.

But from an early age I had developed a habit of being accountable to others, and that is what carried me through in place of a daily writing habit. It was unthinkable that I would not keep a promise that I had made to someone else.

Some people are able to submit a draft of a book in its entirety on the due date. I would not have been capable of this. My editor wisely gave me deadlines that were roughly a month apart.

Writing a book can be uncomfortable and downright painful. Always I reached a point where I was flinging myself over an abyss. If I had not been accountable to my editor and had a deadline, I would have stayed on the other side of the cliff and this book would have remained unfinished. Where habits had failed to stake a claim, deadlines marched in with their demands. Panic and dread were my friends.

According to Dictionary.com, a deadline was formerly "a boundary around a military prison beyond which a prisoner could not venture without risk of being shot by the guards."

Deadlines contain an implied threat—if you don't do this, you are dead. They mark the death of your future self. There is a sense of mortality in deadlines, and that is why they are so effective. There is a kind of death that occurs on the way from the vague to the specific.

When I had an entire day free to write I did not usually start writing until the evening. I only really got going as the monthly deadline, set by my editor, approached. And I did not start writing a book until I was in my fifties, when my mortality truly became real to me. To write this book, I needed to know that time was running out—in the day, in the month, in my life.

After the first three chapters I realized that I had developed a monthly, as opposed to a daily, routine. During later chapters I was able to recognize the peculiar evolution of this routine, which was molded in part by my weaknesses, but also by my strengths.

First would come five to seven days of reading on the topic, and almost no writing. Partly I was researching and incubating, but partly I was also procrastinating. Then, after interviewing people, I would plan to sit down to write—but not write. Eventually I would begin to panic, which in retrospect was part of the routine. Then I would think, "I will get this done. I did it last time." And that's when I did start writing in the morning, and in the evening, and on my lunch hour, and on the weekend.

I have come to realize that the most important thing to do in order to finish a big creative project is this: understand what motivates you, and create a structure to support that.

For me, and for many others, that motivator will turn out to be deadlines and accountability.

Now you may be saying: How nice for this author that she had an agent and a book contract with a deadline. Not all of us with Big Things are lucky enough to have that kind of built-in accountability. For decades I also did not have that, and as I said earlier, I believe I eventually created a situation where I did have it. You can create such a situation, too. That is what Chris Baty did. On May 30, 1999, he sent out the following email to friends and acquaintances around the country:

Here ye! Here ye! Come one, come all, and dust off those word-processing devices! Under the motto "A lousy novel is better than no novel at all," I have declared July National Novel-Writing Month.

To celebrate, I want to write a novel. In a month. And I want you to write one too.

Everybody's got a ton of stories in them. Collectively we have lived over 700 years, and in that time we've accumulated enough characters, places, and plot twists to fill a dozen tomes.

I am proposing that we seize art by the horns, and spill some of those experiences onto the page.

This will be a great exercise for everyone interested in storytelling who has thought fleetingly about writing a novel but has been scared away by the time and effort involved. As you write, you can draw comfort from the fact that, all around the country other National Novel-Writing Month participants are going through the same joys and sorrows of producing the Frenetic American Novel.

Because the writing time is so short, the only thing we're looking for is length. Reach 200 pages (just 7 pages a day!) and you're done! Quality is of no concern. Don't have an ending? Just stop writing at page 200—real writers do it all the time! No plot? No worries! Some of the best novels of the past 20 years haven't had plots.

I think all of us will surprise ourselves with what we are able to produce in such a limited window of time. The short working period will prevent the second-guessing and foot-dragging that can stifle creativity. It will also limit the "I should really be working on my novel" guilt to a one-month window.

To Baty's surprise, twenty people joined him in signing up for the challenge. Six of them—including Baty—ended up finishing a novel. And so National Novel Writing Month was born.

Baty grew up an only child in Kansas City, Missouri, and perhaps significantly, his mother was a psychologist and his father a psychiatrist. His parents nurtured his love of reading. "We had this bookstore policy that any time we went to the bookstore, I could get any book I wanted, which was amazing and nearly the financial ruination of my parents."

Gradually, his love of reading began to evolve into a desire to write. Even as he pursued a degree in anthropology at Stanford, the yearning to write a novel stayed strong. But that seemed like something other people—the novelists—did.

After graduating, he couldn't decide what to do, so he got a job in Portland, Oregon, as a school portrait photography assistant. This was in the mid-1990s, when zines were big. "There was a big, thriving zine community in Portland," he recalled. "Everybody was either in a band or had a zine, and so I started a zine called *Frolic*." He roped his friends into writing pieces for it, and realized how satisfying it was to provide people—himself included—with structure and a deadline, which caused them to become excited about doing something that they wouldn't have done otherwise. A sense of mutual accountability caused the zine and all its pieces to come into being.

Several years later, Baty wanted to see if he could apply the principle of mutual accountability to something much bigger: an entire novel. So he sent out that email. The novel-in-a-month idea immediately lowered the expectations for quality and made it more doable. The idea was "We're probably going to fail miserably, but at least we'll have a good time doing it," he said. "I just wanted to try something and swing for the fences and maybe fail, but that would be okay."

Many of the participants that first year were in the Berkeley area, where Baty now lived. "We would get together after work at coffee shops in Berkeley, and this was back when laptops were ginormous, really the size of small cars, and so it was very unusual at that point to see six people sitting down together at a booth all with laptops, and people were very interested in what was going on there.

"It almost felt at times like we were watching a movie of our novel, and in order to make that movie keep playing, all we had to do was make a lot of typing gestures on our keyboard," he recalled. It reminded him of that moment in *The Lion, the Witch and the Wardrobe* where "those kids discovered that there's this whole other world that they'd been living alongside that they didn't know was there."

He especially remembers a moment with Tim, a cartographer

friend who claimed he hated writing but nevertheless joined the group and ended up completing a novel. Tim was cracking up at the table with tears rolling down his face because one of his characters was doing something crazy.

As Baty had expected, all the novels were deeply flawed—after all, they were just first drafts. But the experience made Baty and his friends realize that creativity for creativity's sake feels wonderful. And they also realized that novels don't have to be written by novelists. They can be written by "everyday people who give themselves time and permission to write novels," Baty said.

If you're going to write a novel in a month, some things have to go by the wayside, and that includes "your own crippling expectations for quality," Baty said. "It's fine to be critical when you have something to review and edit, but if you are constantly second-guessing and analyzing and critiquing every word as you write, you're going to be miserable, so just keep moving. Don't get it right, just get it written. Be assured, it's going to be bad."

Lower your expectations around a finished product right out of the gate and embrace the idea of "exuberant imperfection," he said. Reconnect with that childlike urge to build and create without self-criticism.

"The first draft is so much better if you're not clenching that thing so tightly. You're letting it breathe, and you're making room for spontaneity and weird tangents that sometimes I think end up forming the heart of your favorite parts of the book. All that stuff is so beneficial.

"When you do something big, when you finish something big, even if the result is not beautiful, shining, gilded perfection, simply the act of setting an ambitious challenge for yourself and then nailing it really changes how you see yourself, and it changes how you see yourself as a creative person," he said. People who participate in NaNoWriMo start to ask the question: If I can write a book in a month, what else can I do?

After that first success, Baty moved NaNoWriMo to November,

and instead of the 200-page minimum, switched it to 50,000 words. The word count has great mathematical appeal. Divide 50,000 by the 30 days of November and you get 1,577. That is doable, as long as you don't expect perfection. Lodging that number in my head is what helped me to finally write the first draft of a novel when I participated in NaNoWriMo about seven years ago.

I did not join any of the meet-ups in New York—I wanted to be able to write on my own timetable, and for me writing generally needs to be a solitary activity—but I did tell people far and wide that I planned to write a novel in a month.

That's a secret to success that can be carried over to other big projects, Baty said. "Projects that you are doing quietly by yourself are much easier to abandon. Once you've pulled it out of public view, you have much less incentive to finish it."

What Baty has learned from NaNoWriMo is that "impossible deadlines are easier than merely difficult ones," and they are much easier than lenient deadlines. "I think you need this impossible task in order for you to take it seriously and orient your life around it and then make it this daily project."

NaNoWriMo is proof that even people with full-time jobs and kids and all-around messy lives can still write a novel in a month. In fact, it's easier than if they give themselves five years to do it—during which guilt and misery can accumulate.

Some people can work on a big creative project without a deadline, but in Baty's experience they are a tiny percentage of the population. Realistically, most of these projects are not financially viable, and paying the bills is always going to take precedence. Most people need that sense of fear and accountability.

Is it possible to fail at NaNoWriMo? Baty doesn't think so, although he's had people come up to him, in the manner of a confessor to a priest, admitting that they only wrote, say, six thousand words. "That's six thousand words you wouldn't have written otherwise. You're still having this experience of prioritizing creativity."

But I wondered: "Isn't there's a certain element of narcissism in this?"

Baty's attitude: if it takes some narcissism to get you through this, then that's just fine. It's a perfectly valid motivation to want to impress someone at a party with the fact that you did this.

NaNoWriMo itself became Baty's Big Thing, so that in addition to writing he found himself involved in setting up a Web page and handling fundraising to keep the program and the technology going. It was a crash course in building an organization.

NaNoWriMo now has eight full-time employees at its office in Berkeley. Its Young Writers Program is taught at thousands of schools around the world. A few years ago, Baty gave up his executive director position so he could spend more time writing, but he still serves as a kind of mascot for the program. He continues to do all of the "fun parts of it, which is meeting writers and trying to encourage people to spend more time writing, and none of the actual administrative part of it."

Baty has met people who are now in college who started doing NaNoWriMo in fourth or fifth grade and continue to do it every year, with many of the same people. Part of the appeal is that year after year, people reconnect as a social group. "You develop this close community of people who know each other well at this point and have this shared thing in common that maybe their significant others or their other friends don't share."

But the main thing is, he may be really tired and want to take a night off, but if he sees on the website that there's a group six blocks away meeting to work on their novels, he'll trudge over there and join them. When a group of people are in the same room working on the same thing, it makes the burden so much lighter.

For the people who do it year after year, and that includes Baty, NaNoWriMo is a kind of creative anchor. Whatever crazy, distracting things happen in the other months, there's a commitment to write that novel in November.

In the most recent year, about 350,000 erstwhile novelists around the world participated. And that, some people would say, is not a good thing.

Some literary types have criticized NaNoWriMo, saying it doesn't enhance the overall quality of literature, but instead adds billions of words of drivel to the world. "But I guess I feel like the goal is not at all to improve the quality of literature," Baty said. "I think the goal is to help everybody realize that they have a book in them, and that it is a joyful, fascinating process getting it written." Most people are aware of the realities of the industry and realize that their chances of being published are very small, he said. He tries to get across the idea that "if you do want to publish this, you're at the very start of another long journey." He guesses that maybe 5 to 10 percent of people go on to revise their novels so they consider them complete.

That said, hundreds of respected and bestselling books began during NaNoWriMo, including *Water for Elephants*, by Sara Gruen; *The Night Circus*, by Erin Morgenstern; and *Wool*, by Hugh Howey.

Baty helped answer my question: How do you create a deadline for a creative project when nobody but you really cares whether you finish it? One answer: find other people who are doing the same thing and join some system of accountability for that.

If you can, be the person who sets up such a system for others. Be like Deborah Hay, a choreographer in Austin, Texas, who made her students sign a one-page contract with her that they would practice a solo of her devising every day for a minimum of three months before performing it publicly.

Hay had become frustrated by a lack of commitment among some of her students. She thought if she used a lot of legalese in a paper contract, it would get them to practice—and she would be able to tell if they'd practiced. "I did it because I wanted them to feel official," she told me in an interview.

"You wanted to scare them," I said.

"Scare them and empower them at the same time."

"If they signed the contract and they didn't follow through, what would happen to them? What was the threat?"

"Nothing," she said. But it was effective nonetheless.

The dancers, who came from all over the world, would meet in one place and practice together with Hay for ten days. She would come up with a theme for a solo and coach them in it one by one.

Each solo was the same and yet different. "Everybody was there and saw the response to the feedback as I was giving it to them as they were practicing. Everybody was learning from one another's practice."

Then they would return home and practice for at least three months before performing their version of the solo, as devised by Hay, in a public performance.

There was also a commissioning fee—it started out at around eight hundred dollars—and you couldn't pay it out of your own pocket. You had to get members of your community—relatives, friends, others—to contribute. This was another way to build in accountability.

We need accountability because it's in our nature to behave in ways that do not line up with our long-term interests, said Dan Ariely, a professor of psychology and behavioral economics at Duke University and author of *Predictably Irrational*. Life is full of short-term temptations—and more temptations than ever before.

Some accountability strategies, like Baty's, are full of positive vibrations, but you may need to try a more punishing option. For example, Ariely suggested, try writing out a check to an organization you abhor and ask a friend to send it out if you fail to meet your goal. Or enlist your friends to assist you in various methods of public shaming, such as announcing your failures on social media.

It is possible to take steps to be accountable to yourself, Ariely said. This must start with strict and specific rules. "The rules you want to make are so clear that they are like religious rules," he said. For example, make it an ironclad rule that you are going to sit at your computer—with no Facebook, email, or other websites allowed—from 7 to 9 a.m. with interruptions only for short breaks, and that you will work on a specific part of a specific project. Put a piece of paper on your desk with the date on it, and if you violate your rule, write down "VIOLATION" in big letters. And when you do meet your goal, give yourself a reward.

Another trick is to practice "active no," Ariely said. Tell yourself that if you do not start writing at 7 a.m., you will not write at all for the whole day. Most of the time when we say we don't want to work on something, we actually mean we don't want to work on it *right now* (passing the buck to our future selves). If we can abide by the "active no," we end up being much more thoughtful and disciplined about our work.

"Part of the problem with big projects is we don't see our progress," Ariely said. "So we engage in behavior known as structured procrastination." This is short-term activity—answering email is a prime example—that gives us the feeling of progress and completion we so often lack with our long-term efforts. (Doing the laundry or reorganizing a closet would also fall into this category.)

If you are working on a computer, it can be too hard to literally grasp how much you have done. So find concrete ways to mark your progress—the way I did when I printed out the pages of my manuscript.

"Because the truth is, we need help," Ariely said.

One week, when I was in the midst of revisions on this book, my editor was busy and hadn't given me my next deadline. I could have taken almost an entire week off without doing any work. I thought, How can I make myself work even when nobody will know or care if I haven't? I finally tested an idea that I had long wanted to try:

paying someone to give me encouragement calls. As far as I can tell, there isn't a dedicated place on the Internet to ask for this service. The closest I could come was the gigs section of Craigslist under the subheading "writing." In that section I placed the following ad:

> I am writing a book and need someone to call me next week every day from Monday through Friday—first at 7 a.m. to make sure I start working on it, and then again at 9 a.m. to confirm that I have been working that whole time (except for some short breaks). I am a terrible procrastinator, and I need someone to hold me accountable. I will pay $200 for this service.

I received about eighty responses to my ad—some from professional writers and editors with impressive credentials who offered to read and critique my work as part of the fee, and others from people whose main qualification was that they could really use the money. A few people took a threatening approach: "Stop procrastinating," said one. "It's now or never. People get hit by cars and whatnot every day. I'll call you every day and bug the living hell out of you if you aren't writing."

Another applicant said: "I have zero patience for procrastination and absolutely no sympathy for people who cannot force themselves to sit down at a desk and write, so I am an ideal candidate for this: your excuses, if you are foolish enough to give me any, will fall on deaf ears. Should you tell me that you have failed to write, I think you should pay a tax on it: an additional $50.00 ($25.00 an hour). Want to get something done? Email me and we'll do this. Want to get nothing done? Hire someone else or keep doing what you're doing."

I was tempted to go with the drill sergeant, but in the end one response proved irresistible:

> If you don't mind your encouragement calls coming from across the country, I'd love to call and encourage you. Though we have

a 3 hour time difference, I'm up at 4:00 a.m. milking cows, and can give you a morning call to make sure you are working away before I head to the barn.

At 9:00 a.m. your time, it's 6 here in Washington, and I'll be finishing up my writing time and getting ready for my 7 kids to wake up. Calling again would be the perfect transition for me. Thanks, Lisa.

My first thought was, Is this person for real? I sent her an email and she said her full name was Lisa Tanner. She directed me to a website about her dairy farm that convinced me she was indeed who she said she was. But why, I asked her, if she was a dairy farmer in Washington State, was she perusing the writing gigs section of Craigslist New York? She explained that she was also a freelance writer and that she had been successful getting home-based writing jobs by checking the Craigslist boards for New York and San Francisco. Satisfied with her explanation and charmed by her story, I sent her two hundred dollars via PayPal and instructed her to call me at 7 a.m. the following Monday.

The night before, I was nervous and set my alarm for 6:30 so I would be awake and ready for Lisa Tanner's call. From 6:30 to 7 I lay in my bed in a state of nervous anticipation. At 7:00 sharp my phone rang. "Hi, Phyllis!" Tanner said cheerily. "What are you going to write about today?" I explained that I was going to revise and tighten a chapter that didn't seem to have a clear focus yet. She said she was about to go to the barn and milk her two cows, Maggie and Annie. She promised to call back in two hours to make sure I had done my work. As a result, I sat down and worked on my book for two hours.

At 9 a.m. my time Tanner called me again and said, "Hi, Phyllis. Do you have a focus for your chapter?"

I said I did and asked her how her cows were. She said they were very good.

"Why do you have to get up so early to milk your cows?" I asked.

She explained that it's best to get the milking done before her husband wakes up at five to go to work and before any of her children have gotten up. Her children, she said, are 13, 9, 7, 5, 3, 2, and seven months old, and she homeschools them.

The next day I was a little less nervous but still set the alarm a half-hour early in readiness for my encouragement call. After Tanner called and I explained what I would be working on, I asked her a little more about her farm. She said it was a third-generation farm, started by her grandparents, located about forty-five miles north of Spokane. As she spoke, I could hear a creaking sound, which she explained was the cows on the way to their feeding troughs, passing through thirty-year-old metal stanchions that had been installed by her parents.

The next day I asked Tanner what would happen if she didn't milk the cows. She said that she could possibly skip a day, but if she neglected them for any longer than that, they might get an infection. Now that was a real motivation to get up and work, as opposed to the artificial one I had devised for myself by paying her to call me.

Still, the encouragement calls were working—although on Thursday I was still in bed when Tanner called. "I don't feel like getting up," I grumbled beneath the covers. "Now we can't have that," she said, in a tone I had a feeling she also used with her children. "You need to get up and start writing!" I was ashamed of myself knowing that it was 4 a.m. where she was. And so while still on the phone with her, I hauled myself out of bed and sat down at my computer.

Friday was the last day of the experiment and I wanted to end it on a positive note, so at 6:54 I got to my computer and started working, while bracing for Tanner's 7:00 call. And . . . it didn't come. I continued to write but it was hard to concentrate as I wondered uneasily what had happened. Was she okay? It simply wasn't possible that she would shirk her duty to call me.

Finally, at a little after eight, the phone rang. "I'm so sorry!" she said. "One of my kids was sick last night and we were sleeping on the couch and I didn't take my cell phone with me." She called again at nine and offered to make an extra call on another day, but I said that wasn't necessary.

The next day I called Tanner for a debriefing on the whole experience. A rooster crowed intermittently in the background as we talked. She said she had been nervous about the prospect of calling me because she actually has a bit of a phobia around talking on the phone, but she quickly became comfortable with her role.

Tanner, thirty-one, has a master's degree in education and taught for seven years before devoting herself to the farm, her writing, and teaching her own children at home. The farm is basically a hobby farm and doesn't bring in enough money to support the family. She said she is doing freelance gigs so that one day her husband, a photographer, doesn't have to commute forty-five minutes to his job at an auto repair shop in Spokane. In addition to pursuing photography, he also wants to become a minister.

I asked Tanner if she is religious. She is a Baptist, she said, and was saved when she was eighteen. Her husband (then her fiancé) was also saved around that time.

"Is that why you have so many children?"

"Our philosophy is that the Bible says that children are a blessing and that the Lord is the one who opens and closes the womb," she said. "We're very thankful for the children we have, and we would gladly welcome more. And if we don't we're fine with that, too."

Talk about a legacy. It is Tanner's hope that at least one of their children will want to take over the farm that her grandparents started. The children feed the animals and help with other chores. It gives them a purpose in life, she said, as opposed to just sitting and watching TV.

Tanner's own Big Thing is related to children and teaching. She and her mother, a former kindergarten teacher, are creating an online video course aimed at teaching parents how to teach their children to read.

I asked her if she was aware of any formal setup where somebody can call someone else and encourage them to work on their project. She said she wasn't.

"Do you think the money that I paid was too much? Just in retrospect."

"I felt like it was probably high," she said.

"I felt that way, too—that I could have paid fifty dollars, or at least a hundred. Oh well, I'm happy to help you get your man back home."

As I concluded my highly successful week of paying someone to hold me accountable, I wondered why there was no website dedicated to this sort of thing. Could someone please start one? Until then, if you want to try something like this yourself, the gigs section of Craigslist will work fine. Just don't pay too much the way I did, although it's possible that by paying more I had more skin in the game, so to speak, and therefore worked harder.

Then again, you don't have to pay anything at all. Instead, you could find someone else who is working on a Big Thing and hold each other accountable. It could be a friend, an acquaintance, or a total stranger. In my case, I decided to ask another person who had responded to my ad—a woman named Karen, of Brooklyn, who said that she was writing a book, too. She agreed to be my accountability partner for a week in a barter arrangement.

Karen said in a second email that she was writing an autobiography called "Scandalous." "I lived a very wild life when I was younger," she explained (which is why she didn't want me to use her last name in this book). "I have started writing it several times during the years and lost it on the computer once and another time I wrote it by hand and lost that and I got discouraged and put it off for a while then started again."

I asked Karen if she would be willing to experiment with both phone calls and texting and she was agreeable to that. On Monday, feeling accountable to Karen, I called her at 7 a.m. and asked her what she planned to write about. She said the civil rights movement and Woodstock and free love. I sat down and revised another chapter.

The next day Karen called me at seven and said she planned to write about a job she used to have at the post office that was very dusty. I told her I intended to revise another chapter.

Wednesday was the day that Karen and I had agreed to switch over to texting. I texted her: "Hi Karen, are you ready to start writing?" Followed by a smiley face emoji.

She replied: "Hi! I am sorry. I forgot I have to go to work this morning. So I cannot write but I will be able to write again tomorrow morning."

I went right back to bed.

Thursday morning Karen texted me: "Good morning. It's time to write."

"I am getting up now to work on Chapter 7!" I replied.

"That's good," she said. "I am not sure what I am going to write about yet!"

"That's ok. Just get your ass in that chair! Check back at 9?"

"Lol," Karen said.

At nine Karen texted: "Ok it's 9 a.m."

"Yes, we can stop!" I answered. "What did you end up writing about?"

"Abortion."

On Friday we returned to voice calls, and in our follow-up conversation about the experience, we agreed that the voice calls had been better at motivating us.

I wanted to learn more about Karen, who told me that she was a medical secretary and had an adult daughter. To make extra money for Christmas she was also temporarily working nights cleaning an office, and on Friday she had been too sleepy to write much.

Karen was fifty-eight, divorced from her first husband, and about to divorce her second husband. She grew up in a nice home and her parents tried to send her to college, but instead she dropped out and started fooling around with older men ("I was man crazy") and taking every drug imaginable. That's what everyone on television was doing, so she wanted to do it, too. Finally, she said, she found God through a nondenominational Christian church, and her head became clear. "And then I started to work in the church and help other people like me."

"What is the main reason you want to write your memoir?" I asked her. "To make sense of your life? To help other people?"

"Because there's a lot of people like me out there that think that there's no way to change. They think that they're having fun and then later on in life you see that it's not fun. We need some discipline in our lives. I didn't realize that back then. I wanted to have fun all the time."

"Writing a book gives you discipline," I said.

"Yes, it does. Maybe that's why I'm having trouble."

"Everyone has trouble," I said.

As I tried to work on my Big Thing, it was so easy to become distracted. As Earl Miller, the neuroscientist at MIT, had explained, this was only natural—it was the primitive part of my brain telling me to stop working and watch out for dangerous lions and tigers on the savanna. But then the more evolved part of my brain would step in and tell me to get back to work on this project with a long-term future.

Working on a Big Thing caused me to activate related and meaningful thoughts in my brain. There was a difference in my life while I was working on this book. I had a purpose. As a result, I became involved in moments that were linked, moments that I controlled, rather than outside forces controlling me. These moments, controlled and connected by me, added up to a structure.

Big Things are a strange alchemy of the practical and the spiritual—practical because you must take realistic, incremental, workaday steps to get it done. Spiritual because it calls to some deep part of yourself—a place in the mind, or should I say the soul, where neuroscientists can't go.

I am not a religious person. I have always been an agnostic. If I have believed anything, it is that I don't have enough information to know what to believe. I have always wondered, as the melancholy writer of the book of Ecclesiastes wonders, why we have been given a "sense of time past and future, but no comprehension of God's work from beginning to end."

For people who are religious, faith can carry them over the abyss of doubt. Deep religious faith helped Sherri Kirkpatrick persevere in creating a nonprofit. It helped Dilshad Ali find new ways to reach her autistic son. It gave Linval Thomas the conviction that he would one day record an album. It helped Lisa Tanner and Karen find purpose in their lives.

I don't have that kind of faith, but embedded within the posture lessons and mindfulness classes I took was the basis for a spirituality that I have still dimly grasped but know is there. It expresses itself in the paradoxes of Buddhism.

Yes, I was often distracted, but always I returned to the Big Thing. Whereas before the book, my mind would go hither and thither, alighting on various thoughts, worries, and stimuli with little connection to each other, the book served as a kind of mental tether, pulling me back to my area of focus. Whether the book turns out to be good or not, this mental discipline and concentration was good for me. It gave me purpose and meaning.

It reminded me of what my mindfulness teacher, Paulette Graf, teaches: we always have the potential to begin again.

The building where the mindfulness class was held was not very peaceful. It had no doorman, and the teacher had to let everyone in individually after they rang a loud buzzer. A few people were usually late, after we had begun our initial meditation. My eyelids would flutter open to see who the offending party was. It was spring, and as the weather got warmer, the open windows let in sounds from the street and sidewalk—sirens, children and parents shouting, teenagers laughing. Halfway through the class people who were showing up at the building to take tango lessons in the room below started ringing the buzzer to be let in, and soon the sound of tango music would reach our ears. Not only that, but I almost never did the assignments.

But that was the point of going. At least when I was in the class, I did sit still and try to concentrate on the in-and-out of my breath. Sometimes I did not succeed at this, but other times I did. I see a parallel with writing this book.

I felt I was a failure at meditating, and judging myself to be bad at it made me even worse because you were supposed to be doing it without judgment. A key to mindfulness and to embarking on a Big Thing is to withhold judgment. Chris Baty has shown what turning off self-judgment, while encouraging accountability, can do.

Just by taking on this endeavor, by involving my brain in this complex task, I have done something worthwhile, regardless of how it is received. I have given both my conscious and unconscious mind a focus. What did my mind give up in the process? The possibility of going anywhere at all, which is an illusory freedom. Those endless threads of thought never connect up anywhere. They lead to a diffuseness of experience that is unsatisfying. A Big Thing offers a way toward extended control of one's consciousness. A job offers that, too, but the final goal is ultimately someone else's. With a Big Thing, the goal is your own.

In mindfulness, the goal is to return to the present moment, to take note of distractions and bring yourself back, over and over. It is a very simple concept, but very hard to do.

Similarly, over a period of days, weeks, months, if you are

committed to your Big Thing, you bring yourself back to it. It's hard to do, and you do it imperfectly, but you do it. The Big Thing is an accumulation of the moments where you brought yourself back to the thing you decided to create because it was meaningful to you. And because I always did bring myself back to those moments, I finally got mine done.

Acknowledgments

I *owe the existence* of this book to my agent, Jud Laghi, who contacted me out of the blue to see if I had ever considered working on a book project. He helped turn an underdeveloped proposal that I had already written into a more substantive one, which caught the eye of Hollis Heimbouch, my editor at Harper. Hollis understood the quirky nature of my book from the start and helped me turn it into something more wide-ranging, complex, and personal than I could have imagined. I truly can't imagine a better editor to have guided me through this process. Many thanks also to Eric Meyers, Joanna Pinsker, Fritz Metsch, and the entire team at HarperCollins.

Thanks to my incredibly supportive colleagues at the *New York Times,* including Jeff Sommer, Vera Titunik, Natasha Singer, Dean Murphy, Ken Jaworowski, and Minh Uong, along with Dan Adkison, Dan Cooreman, and Scott Garapolo.

I am grateful to Meg Ciccantelli, Keith Fernandes, Bryan Gieseke, Helen LaFave, Anne Lindeberg, Linda Thrane, and Nia Wronski for their friendship and encouragement during the writing of this book, along with members of my family: Bob and JoAnne Korkki, Jan Leathers, Curt Korkki, and Jean Johnson.

The following people also helped me bring this book to completion in much-appreciated ways: Marci Alboher, Judy Arginteanu, Barbara Balgaard, Isabella Bick, Judith Yates Borger, Carly Bourne, Ada Brunstein, Aanchal Dhar, Joe Eisenberg, Herminia Ibarra, CarolLee Kidd, Tim Kim, Gabriel Koepp, Daniel J. Levitin, Claire Martin, Patricia R. Olsen, Nick Prevas, Heidi Raschke, Hannah Seligson, Charlaine Skeel, Ruth Weleczki, and Ben Yarmolinsky.

And finally, a big hug to the lively ladies of my book club: Paula Cohen, Sara Erickson, Catherine Hogan-Conlon, Ruth Luwisch, Geraldine McGinty, Ilene Kelman, Lisa Kelman, Maura May, Kay Murray, Deanna Retzer, Randi Roberts, Rosemarie Ryan, and Felicia Stingone. Thank you for helping me keep the dream of this book alive.

Notes

Introduction

ix Then a few years ago: The column I wrote was called "Need Motivation? Declare a Deadline," *New York Times*, April 20, 2013.

ONE: The Value of the Long Arc

2 Nancy Molitor, a psychotherapist: From a phone interview with Molitor on September 8, 2014.

4 May makes a distinction: Rollo May, *The Courage to Create* (New York: Norton, 1994), 39.

6 This is a normal human tendency: From a phone interview with Earl Miller on August 3, 2015.

8 One woman I talked to: From a phone interview on September 1, 2014.

9 As the Danish philosopher Søren Kierkegaard wrote: *The Concept of Anxiety*, 1844.

10 Christine Tappolet, a philosophy professor: From a chapter in *The Thief of Time: Philosophical Essays on Procrastination*, edited by Chrisoula Andreou and Mark D. White (Oxford: Oxford University Press, 2010), 125.

11 I have long berated myself: Virginia Woolf, *The Voyage Out* (New York: Harcourt Brace Jovanovich, 1920), 33.

13 According to the results of a large survey: Roy F. Baumeister, Kathleen D. Vohs, Jennifer L. Aaker, and Emily N. Garbinsky, "Some Key Differences Between a Happy Life and a Meaningful Life," *Journal of Positive Psychology* 8, no. 6 (2013).

13 Rollo May uses the word *joy*: May, *The Courage to Create*, 45.

14 Goethe, in *Faust*: J. W. von Goethe, *Faust*, 1808, translated by Charles E. Passage, Library of Liberal Arts (Indianapolis: Bobbs-Merrill, 1965), 42.

16 As Roy Baumeister and John Tierney write: *Willpower: Rediscovering the Greatest Human Strength* (New York: Penguin Press, 2011), 35.

16 "When people have to make a big change": Ibid., 38.

16 The groundbreaking American psychologist: William James, *The Principles of Psychology*, vol. 1 (New York: Dover, 1890), 105–6.

17 By deciding to "launch ourselves": Ibid., 123.

17 "Never suffer an exception to occur": Ibid.

17 Recent neuroscience has confirmed: Charles Duhigg, *The Power of Habit* (New York: Random House, 2012), 15.

17 I no longer have the plasticity of youth: James, *The Principles of Psychology*, 121.

18 Rollo May lays on the guilt trip pretty thick: May, *The Courage to Create*, 12–13.

18 As May puts it: Ibid., 65.

TWO: Mind and Body

20 I decided to take a breathing class: I took the class with Belisa Vranich on October 13, 2014.

24 "Imagine the top of your head": Comments from Lindsay Newitter come from lessons from and interviews with her on October 9 and 22, 2014.

27 Alan Hedge, an ergonomics professor: From a phone interview on October 9, 2014.

29 But when I consulted Mason Currey's book: Mason Currey, *Daily Rituals: How Artists Work* (New York: Knopf, 2014), 84.

29 Heeding his advice: From a home visit by Lindsay Newitter on November 1, 2014.

31 "I don't know if I can do this": From my trip to Scottsdale to visit Dr. James Levine, October 27, 2014.

32 "Every day I climb the mountain": From a phone interview with Dr. James Levine on October 7, 2014.

36 But his colleague, Elizabeth Capaldi Phillips: From an interview with her on October 27, 2014.

THREE: In Bed with the Big Thing

39 And in fact she said that this was the first time: From a home visit by Lindsay Newitter on April 1, 2015.

41 Albaret wrote that he used his illness: Céleste Albaret, *Monsieur Proust*, translated by Barbara Bray (New York: McGraw-Hill, 1976), 67.

41 "The miracle with M. Proust was his will power": Ibid., 65.

41 "The filter was packed tight": Ibid., 22.

41 "the curtains were kept hermetically sealed": Ibid., 49.

42 "but I knew very well that as he lay there": Ibid., 68.

42 "I lie in a chaos of tangled sheets": From a blog post by Charles Simic, "My Secret," *New York Review of Books*, posted February 10, 2012.

42 Most definitely, said Matthew Walker: From a phone interview with him on April 7, 2015.

45 From the time he was a boy: From a phone interview with Dr. James Levine on April 3, 2015.

47 Born in 1981 into a middle-class California family: From a phone interview with Jean-Paul Garnier on April 14, 2015.

51 When I try to record one of my dreams: From a phone interview with Deirdre Barrett on April 10, 2015.

51 Barrett describes several dream "incubation rituals": Deirdre Barrett, *The Committee of Sleep: How Artists, Scientists and Athletes Use Their Dreams for Creative Problem Solving—and How You Can Too* ([N.p.]: Oneroi Press, 2001), 120.

54 Psychoanalysis has gone through many iterations: From an interview with Anne Cutler on April 13, 2015.

59 "For many years I derived self-worth and satisfaction from actively cheating sleep": Julie Flygare, *Wide Awake and Dreaming* (Arlington, VA: Mill Pond Swan, 2012), 56.

59 All of the things that she had been experiencing: From a phone interview with Julie Flygare on April 11, 2015.

FOUR: The Intensity of Illness

63 He felt an instant connection to the painting: From a phone interview with Dr. Fernando Antelo on February 22, 2015.

64 The novelist Carlos Fuentes: *The Diary of Frida Kahlo: An Intimate Self-Portrait*, Introduction by Carlos Fuentes (New York: Abrams, 2005), 11–12.

64 "Through her art": Ibid., 16.

64 "It seemed impossible to me to leave this world": Jan Swafford, *Beethoven: Anguish and Triumph* (New York: Houghton Mifflin Harcourt, 2014), 303.

65 He also "had a sense of virtual hearing through his fingers": Ibid., 719.

65 "much of his late music has an unbroken flow": Ibid., 719–20.

65 As Wil S. Hylton described in a profile of her: The profile by Hylton is titled "The Unbreakable Laura Hillenbrand," *New York Times Magazine*, December 18, 2014.

67 "The work was done in a tightly regimented way": From a phone interview with Janet Browne on February 9, 2015.

69 In fact, studies have shown that writing about your feelings: Tori Rodriguez, "Writing Can Help Injuries Heal Faster," *Scientific American*, November 1, 2013.

69 "creative work can act not only as a means of escape from pain": Kay Redfield Jamison, *Touched with Fire* (New York: Free Press, 1996), 123.

70 "tension and transition between changing mood states": Ibid., 6.

70 She describes herself: From a phone interview with Susan Raeburn on February 19, 2015.

72 "Why can't we acknowledge": Cat Marnell, "On the Death of Whitney Houston: Why I Won't Ever Shut Up About My Drug Use," *xoJane*, February 13, 2012.

72 Although Marnell had received: From an interview on February 11, 2015.

76 At age twelve, she began to have intrusive thoughts: From a phone interview with Elizabeth McIngvale-Cegelski on February 13, 2015.

79 affixed to people like a scarlet letter: Jill Yesko, "An Alternative to ABD," *Inside Higher Ed*, July 25, 2014.

79 When I first talked to her she was five years in and getting closer: From a phone interview on September 1, 2014.

80 At her lowest point, Diane began having panic attacks: From a phone interview on September 4, 2014.

81 It's common for Ph.D. students to experience anxiety and depression: From a phone interview with Anthony Tasso on February 18, 2015.

FIVE: It's About the Experience

85 "I don't feel normal if I'm not making something": From a phone interview with Taylor Harris and Jeroson Williams on March 5, 2015.

87 "It was very humbling and stressful and difficult": From a phone interview with Dilshad Ali on March 15, 2015.

90 I noticed that she had a tendency to talk about past events in the present tense: From an interview with Ann Bancroft on March 9, 2015.

97 I started spilling my woe to the doctor: From an interview with Henry Emmons on March 13, 2015.

SIX: Giving Up, for Now or Forever

104 "When we wish, fear, hope, believe, plan": Karen Horney, *Neurosis and Human Growth: The Struggle Toward Self-Realization* (New York: Norton, 1970), 32.

104 To function well, Horney says: Ibid., 35.

104 A neurosis finagles its way around that challenge: Ibid., 39.

106 "Our lives become an elegy to needs unmet": Adam Phillips, *Missing Out: In Praise of the Unlived Life* (New York: Farrar, Straus & Giroux, 2012), xiii.

106 The desire to work on a Big Thing can be very adolescent and narcissistic: From a phone interview with Howard Gardner on September 18, 2014.

107 "I expected most contributors would follow": David Brooks, "The Small Happy Life," *New York Times*, May 29, 2015.

108 As the teacher of the class: From an interview with Paulette Graf on June 5, 2015.

109 "I've never had a strong burning passion": From an interview with Andrea Loukin on June 4, 2015.

110 "I wanted to be that guy": From an interview with Scott Reynolds on June 5, 2015.

112 he began writing a series of columns: Scott C. Reynolds, "Dream Jobs That You're Glad You Didn't Pursue," *McSweeney's*, 2011.

114 When you are intrinsically motivated: From a phone interview with Tim Kasser on June 9, 2015.

SEVEN: Through the Ages

119 "Of course, I had no idea what a Rothko was back then": From a phone interview with Autumn de Forest and Doug de Forest on December 10, 2014.

122 This is the part of the brain that enables us to plan and achieve long-term goals: From a phone interview with Earl Miller on August 3, 2015.

123 but late-onset creativity is common among visionary artists: From an interview with Rebecca Alban Hoffberger on December 4, 2014.

126 Einstein, for example, with his interest in explaining the universe: Howard Gardner, *Creating Minds: An Anatomy of Creativity Seen Through the Lives of Freud, Einstein, Picasso, Stravinsky, Eliot, Graham and Gandhi* (New York: Basic Books, 1993), 10.

126 "families most likely to foster creativity in children": Teresa M. Amabile, *Creativity in Context* (Boulder, CO: Westview Press, 1996), 212–13.

128 Thomas frequently burst into song: From a phone interview on June 3, 2015.

130 "I kept my dreams alive in small projects": From phone interviews with Sherri Kirkpatrick on November 13 and December 10, 2014.

132 Part of it is that they suddenly realize that they can't take time for granted: From a phone interview with Marc Freedman on August 5, 2015.

133 "Picasso's certainty about his art contrasted sharply with Cézanne's doubt": David W. Galenson, *Old Masters and Young Geniuses: The Two Life Cycles of Artistic Creativity* (Princeton, NJ: Princeton University Press, 2006), 10.

133 Radical conceptual innovation: Ibid., 15.

134 "growing awareness of the complexity of their disciplines": Ibid., 182.

134 "As is the case in painting": Ibid., 161.

135 "some young lad who could take a piece of marble": Tom Wolfe, *From Bauhaus to Our House* (New York: Picador, 1981), 45.

135 "lesser thinkers require role models": Amabile, *Creativity in Context*, 188.

136 "At least ten years of steady work at a discipline of craft seem required": Gardner, *Creating Minds*, 32.

136 "The hardware of the brain is far from fixed at birth": Jeffrey M. Schwartz and Sharon Begley, *The Mind and the Brain: Neuroplasticity and the Power of Mental Force* (New York: ReganBooks, 2002), 120.

136 Even the elderly can alter the inner workings of their brains: From a phone interview with Jeffrey Schwartz on December 4, 2014.

137 maybe by the time you are older: Generativity is discussed by Erik H. and Joan M. Erikson in *The Life Cycle Completed* (New York: Norton, 1998).

EIGHT: The Big Thing and Your Day Job

139 "Kafka's job, while imposing an onerous routine": Ernst Pawel, *The Nightmare of Reason: A Life of Franz Kafka* (New York: Farrar, Straus & Giroux, 1984), 174–75.

139 "I find that having a job is one of the best things in the world": Mason Currey, *Daily Rituals: How Artists Work* (New York: Knopf, 2014), 115.

140 "but if I intended to make a profitable business out of my writing": Anthony Trollope, *An Autobiography* (Oxford: Oxford World Classics, 1999), 103.

142 When he first arrived in New York: Philip Glass, *Words Without Music: A Memoir* (New York: Liveright, 2014), 63.

142 "I set a clock on the piano": Ibid., 83–84.

143 "The passengers could be exasperating": Ibid., 273–74.

144 He got as far as his name and the first sentence: From an interview with John Kuchera on May 13, 2015.

148 "People at the time didn't really go to a store and buy clothes": From an interview with Cenia Paredes on May 14, 2015.

151 Friends of someone who has been laid off: From an interview with Barbara Safani on May 7, 2015.

152 "A lot of millennials and Gen Xers are not waiting": From a phone interview with Nancy Molitor on May 7, 2015.

153 One of the biggest commitments she ever made: From an interview with Camilla Webster on May 5, 2015.

NINE: You're Not Alone

159 guilt-prone people are less likely to collaborate in the first place: Scott S. Wiltermuth and Taya R. Cohen, "I'd Only Let You Down: Guilt Proneness and the Avoidance of Harmful Interdependence," *Journal of Personality and Social Psychology*, November 2014.

160 "you have this feeling of being lost in the wilderness": This and other comments from Chordia are from phone interviews conducted on January 5 and 7, 2015.

161 "When to switch between the social part and the antisocial part": From a phone interview with Robert Sutton on December 22, 2014.

161 "I realized that anything to do with Fermat's Last Theorem": "Andrew Wiles on Solving Fermat," pbs.org, posted November 1, 2000.

162 Sutton, citing research by his Stanford colleagues: Deborah H. Gruenfeld and Larissa Z. Tiedens, *Organizational Preferences and Their Consequences*, John Wiley & Sons, published online June 30, 2010.

163 Sutton offers these suggestions: Robert Sutton, "It's Up to You to Start a Good Fight," *Harvard Business Review* website, posted August 3, 2010.

163 People who self-identify as artists: From a phone interview with Kimberly Elsbach on January 19, 2015.

163 when they studied collaborations among a group of designers at a large toy manufacturer: Kimberly D. Elsbach and Francis J. Flynn, "Creative Collaboration and the Self-Concept: A Study of Toy Designers," *Journal of Management Studies*, June 2013.

165 In a jazz improvisation: From a phone interview with Keith Sawyer on January 20, 2015.

165 This helps usher in a state of "group flow": Keith Sawyer, *Group Genius: The Creative Power of Collaboration* (New York: Basic Books, 2007), 49.

166 The play by Knee that I saw in the making: The rehearsal I attended was on January 6, 2015.

167 "I didn't know where we were going when we began": From an interview with Allan Knee, Michael Roberts, and Thomas Cote on February 4, 2015.

169 I interviewed them separately: My phone interview with Knee was on October 19, 2015. My interview with Roberts was on October 29, 2015.

170 "takes the lone-genius spotlight": Joshua Wolf Shenk, *Powers of Two: Finding the Essence of Innovation in Creative Pairs* (New York: Eamon Dolan Houghton Mifflin Harcourt, 2014), xvii.

171 "Great innovations are usually the result": Walter Isaacson, *The Innovators: How a Group of Hackers, Geniuses, and Geeks Created the Digital Revolution* (New York: Simon & Schuster, 2014), 84.

171 "When people take insights from multiple sources": Ibid., 68.

172 "at least I think his name was Pavel": This and other comments from Prerna Gupta are from an in-person interview on September 25, 2014, and a phone interview on December 29, 2014.

175 In Hollywood, filmmaking began: From a phone interview with Jeremy Braddock on January 16, 2015.

176 For the most part, directors simply cannot carry off the role of "auteur": From a phone interview with Ed Catmull on January 20, 2015.

176 "without the critical ingredient that is candor": Ed Catmull with Amy Wallace, *Creativity, Inc.: Overcoming the Unseen Forces That Stand in the Way of True Inspiration* (New York: Random House, 2014), 87.

TEN: Love and Work

179 Love and work are central to our humanness: Neil J. Smelser and Erik H. Erikson, eds., *Themes of Work and Love in Adulthood* (Cambridge, MA: Harvard University Press, 1980), 4.

179 "Love is an act of imagination": Ethel Person, *Dreams of Love and Fateful Encounters* (Washington, DC: American Psychiatric Publishing, 2007), xx.

179 "allows us both to renew and transform ourselves": Ibid., 5.

179 "One of the things that brought us together": From an interview with Jack Roberts on August 6, 2015.

182 Sherman asked me about my process: From a session with Paulette Sherman on June 18, 2015.

184 "You can be casual and not have horrible posture": From a lesson with Lindsay Newitter on June 29, 2015.

189 I wanted to see how the Shinoharas were doing: I met with the Shinoharas on June 21, 2015.

190 "a woman must have money and a room of her own": Virginia Woolf, *A Room of One's Own* (New York: Fountain Press, 1929).

191 "In a grown-up marriage we gradually acquire a rueful tolerance": Judith Viorst, *Grown-Up Marriage: What We Know, Wish We Had Known, and Still Need to Know About Being Married* (New York: Free Press, 2004), 1.

191 "It requires paying attention": Ibid., 25.

191 "Marriage teaches all of us": Ibid., 38.

191 "So now the work begins": Ibid., 43–44.

193 "There's the parenting life of our fantasies": Jennifer Senior, *All Joy and No Fun: The Paradox of Modern Parenthood* (New York: Ecco, 2015), 1.

193 It is "hard enough to achieve": Ibid., 35.

193 "Children strain our everyday lives": Ibid., 6.

193 They "give us structure, purpose, and stronger bonds:" Ibid., 253–54.

194 "my purpose became clearly evident": David Brooks, "Hearts Broken Open," *New York Times*, June 19, 2015.

194 she was forced to get up before dawn to write: Toni Morrison, "The Art of Fiction," *Paris Review*, Fall 1993.

194 The choice of whether to have children: Interview with Parag Chordia and Prerna Gupta on June 18, 2015.

198 As the author Daniel Goleman told me: My article was titled "The Science of Older and Wiser," *New York Times*, March 14, 2014.

ELEVEN: It All Adds Up

205 "We had this bookstore policy": From a phone interview with Chris Baty on July 29, 2015.

210 "I did it because I wanted them to feel official": From a phone interview with Deborah Hay on August 2, 2015.

211 We need accountability: From a phone interview with Dan Ariely on August 8, 2015.

216 She said she had been nervous: From a phone interview with Lisa Tanner on September 28, 2015.

218 who told me that she was a medical secretary: From an interview with Karen on October 10, 2015.

220 I have always wondered: Ecclesiastes 3:11, New English Bible.

About the Author

Phyllis Korkki is an assignment editor and reporter for the *New York Times* Sunday Business section.